THE
MARRIAGE
MIRROR

intimacy   hope

commitment   success

forgiveness   joy   growth

Reflecting God
In Your Marriage

ED & LISA
YOUNG

CREALITY

Ed Young Resources
Published in Dallas, TX by Creality Publishing.

All Scripture quotations, unless otherwise noted, are taken from The Holy Bible, New International Version (North American Edition), copyright © 1973, 1978, 1984 by the International Bible Society. Used by permission of Zondervan Publishing House.

Any emphases or parenthetical comments within Scripture are the author's own.

ISBN 13: 978-1-934146-83-5

Interior Design & Layout: Jason Acker Design

contents

DEDICATION

A GREAT MARRIAGE IS RARE IN TODAY'S CULTURE. Because of that, we would like to dedicate this book to all the marriages that have persevered difficult times and held true to the covenant vows shared before God and friends.

To our parents, Ed and JoBeth Young and Mendel and Elva Lee, thank you for the reflection you have shown us through your commitment to God and to one another. You truly gave us a wonderful foundation upon which to build our walk with God and with each other.

To the many couples who have held true to their marriage because they know that God's way works, thank you for the example you are setting and the legacy you are building.

And to those who are looking for a husband or wife, we salute you for holding the institution of marriage at a high level. You are investing in a priceless commodity and the payoff is supernatural.

Indeed, marriage is a rare jewel which holds a high value. We believe that this is one of the greatest visuals of Christianity in our world. Through these committed marriages, so many others will gain insight into the greatest relationship of all, a personal relationship with Jesus Christ.

INTRODUCTION

June 26, 1982 was a magical day. We were surrounded by beautiful flowers, our best friends and family, and dressed in the finest clothes that money could rent. It was the day that we dreamed about—and it is a day that we will never forget.

The ceremony itself went by fast, much of it in a blur. We recited our vows and did our best to look like we had it together for our "dearly beloved." Finally, the moment arrived and we sealed our vows with a kiss.

Years later, as we look back at that landmark event in our lives, we're more than a little embarrassed by the cheesy wedding pics. We laugh at our outdated hairstyles and goofy grins. Only in the 1980's would a photographer superimpose the bride and the groom as they looked down on their own wedding ceremony from the balcony of the church. How ridiculous is that?

One of the most memorable pictures is the one that was taken as we were leaving the ceremony. Because in that moment, I wasn't thinking about what we had just done and said. I was thinking, *Honeymoon in Hawaii!* I'm not exactly sure what Lisa was thinking, but I couldn't wait to get through the reception line and get onto the plane.

It was finally time to live "happily ever after." We couldn't wait to kick off our perfect marriage with the perfect honeymoon and live the fairy tale life.

And the fairy tale went great…for about a week.

Our beautiful hotel in Hawaii had a gorgeous view, five-star food and maid service. Our only agenda was sun tanning, swimming and, well, you know. It was the perfect week.

And then, we headed back home. Shortly after we got back, we realized that our humble apartment in Houston was a little musty. It had a vastly different view and was quite cramped compared to the spacious suite we'd been staying at in Hawaii.

Very quickly, very rapidly, romance segued into reality. You know what I'm talking about, don't you? We had arrived at the rugged plains of marital reality.

All of a sudden there were bills to pay. We were both trying to finish college and work at the same time. There were thank you notes to write, textbooks to purchase and work schedules to coordinate. Oh yeah, and the maid service didn't make the trip with us back from our honeymoon. Stress mounted, and romance took a backseat.

If you're single, you may be thinking, "Wait a minute. You mean the romance ended that quickly? I'm going to be different. When I get married it is going to be romance 24/7. It is going to be love, love, love, love, love." If you're married, you know exactly what I'm talking about.

I had no idea what I was saying when I said "I do" to Lisa. I didn't know what those words meant—the implications and ramifications—and I certainly didn't realize what I was signing myself up for. Add to the mix work, kids, financial pressure and in-laws, and you have a recipe for reality: cold, hard reality. And I have to admit that I'm still learning the depth and the richness of those lofty vows that were said on that "magical" day.

The same is true with the Christian life.

When I said "I do" to Jesus years ago, I didn't realize where God would take me. I had no idea what Christ would ask me to surrender so I could serve Him. I didn't realize that I would face ridicule for my faith as a young man at Florida State University. I didn't know that God would lead me away from my family to plant a church hundreds of miles from everything that had made me comfortable. I didn't know the loneliness and the pressure I would face as a pastor. Lisa certainly didn't realize the implications of being a pastor's wife.

Can I tell you a secret?

I have not always been happy in my walk with Jesus. I have not always been happy in my marriage, either. "Ed, are you saying you're not happily married?"

Well, Lisa and I have many moments of happiness in our marriage. But we're not happily married, 24/7. If you think that's what marriage is, I hate to burst your bubble, but that's completely unrealistic. And just to end the suspense, so is the fairy tale, "…happily ever after."

However, the great news is that God never intended for us to live happily ever after. And in this short, but powerful book, I want to share some of the things I have learned as a husband, father and pastor in my journey as a married man. And Lisa will share her unique perspective as a married woman and mother of four.

Together, we want to share God's plan for married couples who have already said "I do" and for singles who are heading towards marriage. We want you to see the depth, richness and beauty of the most important earthly relationship you will ever experience. And we want you to see how a marriage between a husband and a wife can reflect the marriage between God and His Church.

Aside from our relationship with Christ, marriage is the best thing Lisa and I have in life. We love our friendship, our partnership. We enjoy the intimacy and connection that we share. Most importantly, we have been blown away by the many ways our marriage has helped us grow as children of God and equipped us to be the salt and light to the watching world around us.

We have a passion to help encourage other couples to discover God's awesome plan for marriage. Our prayer is that this book will help revolutionize the way you view marriage. And as you learn to see God's pure and holy reflection in your own marriage (or future marriage), you will experience all the benefits of committing to one another, loving one another and staying together "till death do you part." And best of all, you'll begin to experience all that God has in store for your life through this beautiful relationship; the only relationship that reflects God's unique relationship to His people.

CHAPTER

HOLLYWOOD, MARRIAGE and THE GOSPEL

CHAPTER 1

HOLLYWOOD, Marriage and THE GOSPEL

Lisa and I have a great marriage. We are more in love today than ever before. Today, we have four beautiful kids, a few Dobermans, and we have been blessed with phenomenal opportunities to serve God together. We love marriage and we have a passion for other couples to discover God's awesome plan for marriage in His plan for us in a covenant.

One of our favorite things to do together is to go to the movies. We love escaping from the house and catching the latest and greatest movie. A lot of times I'll pick a typical guy's movie with lots of action. When Lisa picks the movie, the romantic comedy is often the choice du jour. After more than twenty-five years of marriage I've learned something. And guys, here's some free advice: Let your wife pick the movie. You'll thank me later.

Romantic comedies are interesting (and idyllic, to say the least), because they're all written with the same premise. The biggest blockbuster romantic comedies involve the same people, too.

There's one actor (I won't mention his name) who loves taking his shirt off. I read one time that this particular actor gets paid almost $5 million more when he takes his shirt off in the movie. I can't really blame him; if I had abs like that I'd take the huge paycheck too!

But every movie follows the typical romantic comedy script. It goes something like this: two impossibly beautiful people meet in strange circumstances, fight and the poor sap spends the rest of the movie chasing her down. After a bizarre act of devotion, she takes him back and…are you ready for this…the two live happily ever after. That is a marriage made in Hollywood.

We're all familiar with that silver screen version. But there is a different script when God writes the narrative. And since God invented marriage, I think it would be wise to see what He says about it throughout the pages of Scripture.

In the Bible, God is described as the groom who initiates the covenant relationship of marriage with His bride.

- In the Old Testament, God is described as a generous husband who provides His wife with security and adorns her with fragrant oil and beautiful clothes.[1]

- The Lord is also described as a doting husband who is jealous for the affection and devotion of His wife.[2]

- In the book of Hosea, the ultimate groom pledges His eternal faithfulness, love and compassion to His wife.[3]

- In the New Testament, as God reveals His redemptive plan for the world through the person of His holy Son, Jesus Christ is called the groom and the Church is now described as His bride.

- In similar language, Christ commands modern day husbands to love their wives in the same way as He loves the church and gave Himself up for her.[!]

When you put all of this together, we see that our God is the ultimate groom who initiates the covenant of marriage, protects His wife, provides for her beauty and sacrifices everything to demonstrate His undying love and devotion to her. It is sad to see how Hollywood has softened and hidden this beautiful relationship that mirrors God's relationship to His people.

To take it a step further, a God-centered marriage should mirror the gospel. When you hear the word "gospel," you may think of Billy Graham tracts, or preachers on street corners shouting about the end of the world. You might think about the words "good news" or the message of Easter which describes the gospel as the death, burial and resurrection of Jesus. That's all true.

But when you think about the word "gospel", do you ever consider your marriage? One of the goals of this book is to help you begin linking the gospel message to the concept of your marriage. Marriage is not a fairy tale or a made-for-TV movie. Marriage should mirror God's marriage to His people. Marriage should mirror the death, burial and resurrection of Jesus Christ.

The Nature of God Reflects Oneness

You can't go anywhere these days without experiencing an avalanche of sexual images that vie for your attention. Entire magazines are devoted to mostly (or fully) naked men and women to arouse us, but also to distract us from God's design for intimacy in marriage. Romance novels and cable networks are devoted to tales of men and women coming together for sexual encounters, often at the expense of an existing marriage.

Sooner or later, we have to ask the question, Why? Why are we so enamored with sexual images and stories about intimacy? The answer might surprise you. It is found in one of the most often quoted marriage verses in the Bible.

For this reason a man will leave his father and mother and be united to his wife, and they will become one flesh.[5]

That passage appears in most weddings or sermons about marriage, as the pastor expounds upon the holy and sacred nature of the marriage relationship. What we don't often think about is that this verse lays the foundation for our sexual desire as well. This is the biblical principle of oneness that we can only experience in the marriage bed, but often seek through illicit means.

When you read about God's design for marriage, you learn about His desire for oneness. The math of marriage is one + one = one. One man, one woman following God in a covenant relationship called marriage produces a one flesh relationship.

A covenant is a blood bond of life and death. A covenant is not a flippant promise; in the Bible it required the sacrificial death of unblemished animals. The sealing of the covenant was to say that if one deviates from the terms of their arrangement, may God do to them as has been done to the sacrificial animals.

Oneness is the mysterious concept that attracts us at our deepest level. It is our desire for harmony and unity that lures us all toward meaningful relationships.

Oneness is that desire for true intimacy that escaped the lonely addict while illicit images flash across their computer screen. Oneness is what drives a lonely man or woman to sleep in the wrong bed as they trade sex for the promise of intimacy.

Everywhere you turn throughout the pages of Scripture, you see oneness. You see oneness in the very nature and character of God. The holy Trinity is God the Father, God the Son and God the Holy Spirit moving in concert with one another to accomplish His agenda for the universe. In the Trinity you see equality in form and uniqueness in function. You see the Father delegating to the Son and the Son delegating to the Spirit. In some accounts, all three are present at the same time to demonstrate the complexity and the beauty of God's nature. In others, you'll find one member of the Godhead more active than the others. Throughout the Bible there is no mistaking the mysterious nature of the oneness of God.

We also see oneness in the description of God's desire for the unity of His people. We see it in the description of the nation of Israel and in the emerging church in Acts 2. As we've already seen, oneness was established in the first book of the Bible, Genesis, for the covenant of marriage between a man and woman.

We don't seek sex because we are red-blooded men and women. It's not because we are finally liberated from sexual oppression or because we want to control our own sexual destiny. We don't pursue porn because we are perverted people. We do it because we are desperately seeking God and the oneness that He has imbedded into our DNA. I would argue that the closest you can get to God is being joined together in oneness, through sex, with your spouse. And because many of us are reading the Hollywood script, we are searching for oneness through improper channels. It's our search, it's our desire and it's our passion for oneness that is our ultimate pursuit.

Here is where the gospel and marriage connect.

Jesus has done the work to allow us ultimate connection with God. He has put the cards on the table. He sacrificed and He suffered to provide for us, His bride. His death, burial and resurrection were accomplished to clean us, adorn us with beauty and provide us with eternal security. The work is finished. To experience oneness with God, all we have to do is say, "I do" to Jesus. That's it.

At its essence, the gospel is this: God came to earth in the form of Jesus Christ and lived a perfect, sinless life on this earth. He died a sacrificial death on the cross and then rose again from the grave.

When we accept that truth; when we ask Jesus to be the Lord and Savior of our lives, we have essentially said "I do" to him.

THE GOSPEL IS REFLECTED IN Marriage

A marriage between a man and a woman reflects the gospel. When I die to my selfishness—in other words, when I get off the couch and take out the trash; when I do something to serve my spouse—my marriage goes a lot better. When Lisa dies to her selfishness, we start clicking.

This biggest problem with my marriage is me. The more my marriage becomes a reflection of myself, the more problems I'm going to face. The less I think about myself, the more my marriage reflects the sacrificial death of Jesus Christ.

A lot of us are carrying around baggage from a previous relationship or from a messed up childhood. As we pray through our sin that often ensnares us, we have to allow God to bury our past—and leave it there. That doesn't mean we gloss over our sin; we have to repent and ask God for forgiveness and healing. However, we can't move forward as a husband and wife until each of us has buried our past. The resurrection is what gives us the hope of doing that.

According to Paul, without the resurrection, let's "eat, drink and be merry because tomorrow we die."[6] Life is futile without the reality of Christ's resurrection. The great news, though, is that the power and the hope of the resurrection are on tap for all of us who believe in Christ.[7] It's what gives this one and only life meaning, today and forever.

That means the same power that raised Christ from the dead is available to all of us who are working on our marriages. It is available for our thought life as we strive to protect our minds. It is available to overcome our addictions. It is available for singles who are saving their bodies until they pledge themselves in a covenant marriage before God and their spouse.

The mystery of the gospel is reflected in marriage. It's seen when we realize that we aren't the only ones in the relationship. And it becomes reality when we sacrifice our wants and needs and desires for those of our spouse.

Christ's sacrifice should be on display through our marriage. The power of the living Lord should be evident in our marriages. Grace, mercy and forgiveness should be reflected as people watch your marriage.

We Are Perfected in Marriage

Marriage is the greatest place for you to develop your maturity in Christ. There is no greater place for you to go deeper with God than in your marriage. There is no prayer meeting, Bible study or CD library that can possible equal what will happen to you as you allow God to perfect your salvation through marriage. It is also the best place to see your character built.

Sometimes people ask me, "What type of love is marriage built on? Is it built on hot and passionate love? Is it built on the sappy, dripping off the drapes kind of love?"

There are several types of love mentioned in Scripture that we see in marriage.

The first is eros love. We get the word "erotic" from it. That's the passionate love; that's the sexual love; that's the hot love. That's the honeymoon kind of love you experience that burns for a few days and then flames out when the realities of life set in. It ebbs and flows throughout your marriage. It's also the kind of love that you have to be careful of so you don't get burned. Eros love quickens your pulse, weakens your knees and stirs the butterflies in your stomach. Eros is important for a male-female relationship. You've got to have that *wow* factor. And while eros is important in marriage, it can't be the foundation.

The second kind of love we find in Scripture is phileo love. The city of brotherly love is Philadelphia. Phileo is the friendship factor, the recreational companionship, this ability to talk and just really enjoy the company of your spouse. You've got to have that when you load up the minivan with a gaggle of kids in your backseat asking, "Are we there yet?" We need the friendship of our spouse, because marriage is not always erotic. It doesn't always follow the honeymoon schedule of sun tanning, swimming and, well, you know. Phileo is what allows you to truly enjoy the company of your spouse; it's what makes you call your spouse your "best friend."

Agape love is the love mentioned in Scripture that transcends them all. This is the irrational, unconditional love that God has demonstrated to us.[8] It's the covenant love. It is the kind of love that sacrifices for the good of another. It is selfless. It is relentless. It is supernatural. Without this kind of love, we are doomed to fail. This is what separates the thriving marriage from the status quo marriage. It is what should separate the Christian marriage from the made-for-TV movie marriage.

We've all seen marriages that are built on erotic love. Two vivacious people lock up for the hot, romantic, chills-on-your-spine love. But you can't build a lifelong commitment on erotic love. You show me a marriage that's built on erotic love and I will show you a marriage that will maybe last twenty-four months. Erotic love is a shooting star that burns brightly for a time, but is not sustainable, nor is it the foundation for your marriage. Eros erodes quickly. We need it, but we can't build a marriage on it. Eros doesn't stretch; it just breaks and blows up.

Phileo love is another love you have to have. You have to be able to connect, talk and enjoy each other's company. You can't underestimate the friendship factor in marriage. Recreational companionship (other than sex) is one of the key factors in marital longevity. If you're going to call someone your lifelong companion, you'd better have some activities you enjoy doing together.

Agape love, though, is the foundation God intends for our marriages. It's unconditional, it is always thinking about the other person. It is gospel love. And it's only truly possible when the husband and the wife are committed to the leading of the Holy Spirit in their lives.

Maybe you are having problems in your marriage right now. Only God knows what you are dealing with as you read these pages. I will tell you this right now: no matter how difficult your problems are, they can be overcome supernaturally when you practice agape love. Focus on meeting your spouse's needs and focus your marriage on the gospel of Jesus Christ. If you do that, one day you'll look back and your legacy will stand for eternity. The legacy that you will leave will dominate the passing problems that seem so monumental right now.

Whenever you see a divorce, you're seeing the result of at least one spouse who refuses to allow the gospel to be perfected in their life. When the gospel is not perfecting you and me, we are powerless to build meaningful marriages and lifelong legacies.

That's why I said that marriage is the greatest place for you to grow in your relationship with God. The marriage commitment is all about spiritual maturity. When we grow with God, we can grow with our God-given spouse.

What's the more spiritually mature thing to do? Is it to get up at 4:00 a.m. so you can pray for an hour and study the Scriptures? Or is it to get yourself out of your warm bed to change a dirty diaper so your spouse can sleep? Is real spiritual maturity getting together with your friends to talk about the latest Christian book? Or is it staying home with your spouse who is sick to do nothing in particular but be together?

Let's go ahead and get real for a second here. When you sign up for marriage, you are signing up for a lifelong course in maturity from which you will never graduate. You're signing up for God to build some serious stuff in your life as He holds the mirror of the gospel up to your desires and your actions.

When I look at Lisa, I see my very best. Unfortunately, I also see my very worst. When she looks at me, she sees her best. She also sees her worst. Marriage isn't the easiest thing; it's the hardest thing. But the hardest thing can become the greatest thing when we allow the gospel to be fully formed in our lives as we live it out in the context of our marriage. People are looking at you and they're looking at me and they're dying to catch a glimpse of Jesus. Are they seeing the gospel reflected and perfected in you and your marriage? Are they seeing the holiness of God?

But just as he who called you is holy, so be holy in all you do; for it is written: "Be holy, because I am holy."[9]

That verse says it all. We need to reflect the holiness of God. And marriage is where that is played out. As I read recently in a book, marriage is not necessarily for my happiness; it's for my holiness.[10] Marriage may not give me quiver-in-my-liver kind of fuzzy feelings 24/7, but it will bring joy and contentment as the gospel is perfected in our life together as husband and wife.

WE ARE PROTECTED IN MARRIAGE

A covenant is a blood bond before God. The new covenant for believers in Christ was sealed when the Son of God was raised from the dead. As with other covenants, it was initiated through the sacrifice of blood, Christ's blood on the cross.

The marriage covenant is really a covenant within that covenant. The ultimate covenant is between God and us. The marriage covenant reflects the ultimate marriage. Within the marriage covenant, we have protection.

Many people today are anti-marriage. But they are that way because they misunderstand marriage. They have this whacked out view of God's plan for marriage and they see it as stifling and constricting. People say, "Well I want to be free. I want ultimate freedom. I don't want anything, or anyone, holding me back."

Sadly, the freedom we think we want ultimately leads to chaos. When we think about freedom, we imagine a world where there are no rules, no consequences, no right and no wrong. Somewhere, John Lennon is smiling.

Not long ago, my family and I were vacationing together in the Caribbean. One Tuesday morning we went snorkeling in this beautiful body of water. We were together on this tiny boat and just awestruck by the magnitude and the variety of God's creation. The water was crystal clear and we were able to see fish and wildlife we had never seen before.

But it wasn't long before the title song from my favorite movie started playing in my ears. Da Na. Na Na. Da Na. You remember the movie, *Jaws* don't you? Whenever people go swimming in the ocean, eventually they worry about the monstrous, blood-thirsty shark.

Not wanting to expose my fear in front of my wife and kids, I quietly pulled the snorkel guide aside and said, "Excuse me, are there any sharks in the area? I mean, my kids are worried; not me."

He said, "No, man! See the reef right there? The sharks are on the other side of the reef, so we can be free to swim on this side of the reef."

With those words, I just dove in. We had a great time snorkeling, looking at these eagle rays and all the different fish and eels. We were free to enjoy the wildlife and the water.

When we were snorkeling, we were totally free. Why? Because we were protected within the reef. We were totally free because we were inside the guidelines and the guardrails of the reef.

When it comes to marriage, God has set up a perfect reef. He has built a custom reef for our marriages and He says to us, "Be free in marriage. Express yourself openly within the protection of your covenant. Enjoy the beauty of your relationship as you enjoy the gift of your spouse. Enjoy the eros love, phileo love and agape love. You're free because of this covenant, this relationship I have established for you. My Son laid down His life for your freedom. His death, burial and resurrection are available for your life and it's on tap for your marriage."

Have you responded to Him? Have you said "I do" to Jesus? If you are married, do people see the supernatural power of God in your interactions with your spouse? Does your marriage reflect the gospel? Does the gospel perfect your marriage? Is your marriage protected by the gospel?

God has sought you; He's romanced you and paid the ultimate price for you by sending His Son to do the work on Calvary. And because of His holiness and His supernatural power, He rose again.

So if you want to know what life is all about; if you want to know what the ultimate marriage is all about, say "I do" to Jesus because the implications are unbelievable and eternal.

The gospel is the ultimate love story between a gracious God and His people. Through the truth of the gospel He initiates and provides for our growth. Marriage is about the gospel. It is the place where the mirror of God's agape love allows us the opportunity to showcase the power of God to a watching world. And it's a place where we can mature in our relationship with Christ.

A TIME FOR REFLECTION

GENESIS 2:24

*For this reason a man
will leave his father and mother and
be united to his wife, and
they will become one flesh.*

QUESTIONS:

As you look into the mirror of your marriage, what kind of love do you see reflected most—eros, phileo or agape?

When other people look at your marriage, how will they see the power of the gospel reflected back to them?

_____

_____

_____

_____

_____

_____

_____

_____

_____

_____

_____

_____

_____

_____

_____

_____

_____

_____

_____

_____

_____

_____

_____

CHAPTER 2

A VILLA IN ANGUILLA

A WHILE BACK I WAS INVITED TO SPEAK at two churches on Anguilla, a tiny island located in the Caribbean Ocean. A generous woman who lives there offered to fly my family and me down for a few days and let us stay at her villa—a villa in Anguilla. This place was amazing! It was situated on a hill overlooking the entire island. We had a 360-degree perspective of the vast ocean, with crystal clear water in every direction—the Caribbean on one side and the Atlantic on the other. I'd never seen a view quite like that.

While I there, I was thinking about what God has been teaching me about marriage. And I realized that the villa we were staying in represents perfectly the picture of marriage.

God has given Lisa and me this beautiful structure to live in, a villa that provides us with a place to share our intimacy, connection and love. And it's also gives us access to an incredible 360-degree perspective of the world around us.

Marriage allows me to see more about myself, God and the

world around me. And as we process the mystery and beauty of marriage, I believe God will give us the ability to see the world in deeper and richer ways.

But to get a view that is reflective of what God wants us to see, we have to understand who marriage is for and what it does. Obviously on a simple, basic level, it's between a man and a woman. It's an earthly relationship between two people. But when we focus on just that aspect of marriage, we run into the classic case of the pendulum swinging too far to one direction.

In the recent past, marriages have struggled mightily. The sad reality is that Christ-followers are not immune to the destructive nature of divorce. Divorce leaves a trail of broken homes in its wake. And understandably, that brokenness has left single men and women paralyzed in taking the next step in their own relationships.

I believe there is a general fear of commitment from singles because of the pain and destruction of divorce. As a reaction against divorce, well-meaning psychologists, leaders and speakers have developed personality tests, conferences, CDs, books and a myriad of other pre-marital resources. While those are all well and good in moderation, today's market is flooded with them. And because of that, many people have become even less confident in their decision to get married. They think they have to match perfectly on a test or survey to the person they are dating in order to get married. And because of that, so many are gun shy about saying "I do."

If Lisa and I went through the vigorous personality and compatibility tests, we would have *never* gotten married. There's no way we would have matched perfectly. If we took those tests today, the results would probably tell us that we still wouldn't be a perfect fit.

In a lot of ways, we did things all wrong by today's pop-psychology standards. We got married in our early twenties, while we were still in college. Neither one of us had a stable, full-time job at the time. We hadn't even traveled around the world to "find ourselves." But we didn't focus on what we didn't have. We focused instead on the connection that God had built in our lives. And we took the plunge.

To help correct this obsession with matching perfectly with the other person, let me share with you a very simple biblical requirement for marriage. Let's clear the fog and get back to reality. If you are a Christ-follower and have a desire for the opposite sex, *get married*. All you need is one man who is following Christ, plus one woman who is following Christ who share a desire for the covenant of marriage.

It's not that complicated. And when you follow that requirement and follow God's plan in your marriage, the implications and scope of marriage is that 360-degree perspective that has the power to change you, your spouse and the world that is watching you. And ultimately, you'll discover who marriage is really for.

Now, I'm not saying that you don't need to have some chemistry and compatibility going on, or that you don't do your homework about this other person. That's a subject for another book. In fact, I've written an entire book about dating and finding the right mate, entitled *Rating Your Dating While Waiting for Mating*. In it, I go into great detail about how to date and pursue a marriage partner in a biblical, God-honoring way.

What I am saying is that we often make that process too complex. While we need to spend a lot of time getting to know potential mates—learning their likes and dislikes, getting to know their friends, understanding their temperament, making sure we have common interests, and so on—we often forget that the foundation for a great marriage goes deeper than all that stuff. It is the spiritual connection through Christ.

MARRIAGE IS ABOUT JESUS

In the book of James[1], the Bible is described as a mirror that reflects our hearts and serves as a check-up for our spiritual maturity.

When I see a piece of broccoli stuck in my teeth, I remove it. When my hair looks like a hedgehog, I add a little water to correct the problem.

In marriage, God gives us a big mirror for our spiritual maturity. The marriage mirror is a reflection of the gospel of Christ. It will awaken us to our selfishness, our pride and show us where we are falling short. Other times, the marriage mirror will reflect the grace and power of the gospel when we truly love our spouse like Christ loved the Church.

Marriage should be a beautiful picture that reflects the grace of God. People should see reconciliation in action when they see your marriage. They should see humility. They should see love-in-action through service. To put it plainly, people should see Jesus.

One of the reasons why divorce is so sad is that it distorts the image and reflection of God. When followers of Christ turn their backs on the power of the gospel in their lives and in their marriage, selfishness creeps in and a marriage can shatter. Instead of seeing the difference that a Christian marriage can make, it further buries the wonder, the beauty and the depth of the only relationship that mirrors God's relationship to His people.

The Bible says that when we say "I do" to Jesus, we are adopted into His family. That doesn't seem like a big deal when we read it through the lens of the 21st century. But if we travel back to the time in the 1st century when this term was used in this context, we see why adoption is so significant.

In those days, you could disown your biological child. But

once you adopted a child into your family, you could not turn your back on them; you could not disown that child. When followers of Jesus say, "I do" to Him, God adopts them permanently into His family. And the result is our permanent salvation. We can't be kicked out of the family of God. Theologians call it the "eternal security of the believer."

It reminds me of a time when my twin daughters and I were walking across the street when they were little. I remember holding their tiny hands with a vice grip. As their father, I was much stronger than they were. The more they squirmed, the harder I would squeeze, because I didn't want them to get away and possibly get hurt. No matter how much they tried to wiggle free, I wasn't about to let go. I love them and I want to protect them.

God is the same way. He isn't going to let us go. He's not going to disown us. He is always going to stand by us—even if we try to turn our back on His love and grace. This kind of permanent relationship builds phenomenal security into your life and mine. There is no security like the kind that happens when we know that the Creator and sustainer of the universe will stand by us on our best days—and our worst days.

Because of the mirror that is marriage, we have the opportunity to provide that kind of security for our spouse. When we reflect the unconditional and irrational love that Jesus showed us; when we demonstrate consistency even when our spouse is unlovable; we will build trust that will allow our spouse to truly flourish.

Instead of lashing out when your husband forgets your birthday, show forgiveness. When your wife says, "Not tonight, honey," don't get bent out of shape. Understand her feelings. It is in these brief moments that you can demonstrate to your spouse that your marriage isn't built on fleeting feelings or selfish desires. Rather, use those times to reflect the nature and character of Jesus.

If you've already gone through the pain of divorce, let me say a few words to you. First, divorce is not the unpardonable sin. Our God is the God of second chances and He has proven that through the sacrifice of His one and only Son for sinful people like me and you. You are already facing the consequences of your divorce; you don't need any further proof that divorce is not God's plan for married people.

If you do consider getting remarried, let me challenge you to pay special attention so you can break the cycle of divorce for your family. Take the time to truly heal from your previous marriage before you even think about dating. Too often, I've seen the same set of issues trail divorcees from relationship to relationship. Let me urge you to process what happened and get the necessary Christian counsel to grow through your divorce.

Divorce is not a silver bullet that will solve your marital problems; every marriage deals with sin and the junk and funk that occurs because of our inherent selfishness. That's why the marriage mirror is so important for those who follow Christ. This mirror reflects the reconciliation, forgiveness and power of the gospel. It is others-centered and offers a lifetime of second chances. Where would any of us be if God had not given us another chance through Christ?

God loves you and, if you are a Christ-follower, He has permanently adopted you in His family. He wants to heal you and help you make a difference in this world as you learn to honor Him, and as you realize that your marriage is ultimately for Jesus.

Marriage is About Others

Our marriage is about the mirror reflection of the gospel of Jesus

Christ, and that is especially important as it relates to others who are watching us. Marriage is not just for us; it is for others.

The primary reason why a marriage breaks up is because one or both parties have forgotten the gospel. Either the husband or the wife has forgotten that true maturity is thinking about other people.

Every time you go to a wedding ceremony of a friend or family member, listen to the marriage vows again and take them to heart. They may not be worded exactly like yours were, but the point is the same. Those vows are not just important for the couple getting married. They are also a reminder to every couple listening to keep their vows, because people are watching.

A healthy or unhealthy marriage doesn't just affect you; it also reflects you. It sends a positive or negative message to others. What kind of reflection is your marriage sending to the people in your life, to those who are in your circle of influence? Do they see Christ at the center of your marriage?

Your Spouse

Jesus said there are two, big commandments: Love God with everything and love others as you love yourself.[2]

Our culture is obsessed with *me*. It's all about what makes *me* look good, what makes *me* feel good and what gives *me* pleasure.

But what if marriage isn't about *me*? What if marriage is more for my perfection in Christ than it is for my pleasure?

Your marriage isn't about you. It's not really for you. It's for your spouse. And when your marriage is a true reflection of the gospel, your spouse experiences some powerful stuff. Rather than seeing a self-centered spouse when they look at you, they will see security, unconditional love and the power of the resurrection.

So often, it is the little problems that darken the mirror of marriage. It's when you take the focus off your husband and put it on his dirty laundry. Or when you stop serving your wife and instead worry about the number of days you've gone without sex.

These small issues become greater and greater when they distract us from serving our spouse. When our own needs overshadow what our spouse needs from us, we get into this downward spiral of who-can-be-more-selfish. After we live in this cycle for a while, we start to look outside the marriage for our needs to be met. And that's when affairs—emotional or physical—take place. We start fantasizing about divorce and moving on to another partner when in reality the same problems, the same issues will appear in the next relationship.

When you fantasize about hooking up with that guy from your office or the girl in the health club, do you think about what it will do to your spouse? Do you think about the erosion of security that they will feel? Do you think about sitting across from them in court with tears running down their face? Even worse, how will a divorce affect their view of God and the gospel?

In marriage, we can build amazing security into our spouse. Because of the foundation we have in our relationship with Christ, we can extend security to our partner. The security that Lisa and I have with one another should be reflective of the eternal security that we have in Christ. And when you have that kind of security; when you both have resolved to stay married through the good times and the tough, you are going to discover that security breeds confidence. And confidence breeds excellence. There is nothing like the feeling of knowing that your spouse is beside you come hell or high water.

What are you communicating to your spouse about the gospel?

What are you showing them about forgiveness? How is unconditional love being expressed in your marriage?

Jesus loves us, even when we are the most unlovable. He looked down on the cross with love in His eyes and said, "Father, forgive them. They don't know what they are doing."[3] Jesus loves us even though we're fallen and fallible. Jesus loves us and His love is intentional and it's pursuing and it surrounds us and ambushes us.

That's why God says, *Husbands, love your wives, just as Christ loved the church and gave himself up for her.*[4]

If you're a husband or hoping to be one, don't worry about trying to climb Everest or run a marathon; you already have a monumental challenge laid out for you. This is the command given to every man who is married or thinking about marriage. You're called to reflect Jesus. You're challenged to mirror Jesus to your spouse.

What kind of mirror are you for your wife?

What kind of mirror are you to your husband?

Your Children

Your marriage is for your spouse. It's also for your kids. What is your marriage teaching your kids? Are they seeing forgiveness in action? Are they seeing what it's like to feel totally secure in the arms of another? Are you building discipline and endurance into your children by sticking it out?

Your kids don't need to see the perfection of *Leave it to Beaver*; they need to see the octane of commitment in the form of a marital covenant in action in your marriage.

If you do turn your back on your marriage, you are teaching your kids to bail out when the going gets tough. And studies have shown that kids who came from a family with divorce are more likely to get divorced themselves.

I'm not talking about marriages with abuse or abandonment; those are unique situations. I'm talking about marriages where safety and confidence can be displayed for our children to see.

I learned a long time ago that the best thing I can do for my kids is to work on my marriage. When I love Lisa as Christ loved the Church, I am doing the very best thing for my four kids. When I express selfishness to Lisa, I am eroding their self-esteem.

So goes your marriage, so go your kids. So goes your marriage, so goes your parenting. So goes your marriage, so goes the foundation and the self-esteem and the confidence of your kids. So goes your marriage, so goes the trajectory of your kids when they leave home to live their own lives.

If you are worried about your kids, then worry about your marriage. And do what you can to work on that relationship. There is no better investment you can make into the success of your kids than a healthy and stable marriage.

That is counter-intuitive to what I see many parents doing all around me. These days, parents are often caught in the web of the performance plan with their kids. We are so desperate to keep our kids happy and successful that we will bounce from dance recital to soccer practice to a sleepover, home for some microwave pizza, and then back out for more activities.

Be very careful that you don't allow your children to supersede your relationship with your spouse. I've said for many years that KIDS stands for: Keeping Intimacy at a Distance Successfully. I think that's a great acrostic, I have to admit! I truly believe that our kids can be one of the greatest barriers to marital fulfillment, if they take a front seat in the family. Your marriage has to take priority over your relationship to your kids.

In just a few years, your kids will leave and your spouse will stay. Before you know it, your kids will be graduating and moving out. Be careful that you don't allow your kids to drive a wedge between you and your best friend. Otherwise, you'll be driving back from college orientation with a stranger sitting beside you on a very lonely trip home.

Your marriage is about Jesus. Your marriage is about your spouse. And your marriage is about your kids.

The World

Your marriage is also for the world watching you. What kind of mirror are you reflecting to those outside the family of God? Many people are skeptical about the power of the gospel. Does your marriage showcase the power of Christ's resurrection? Do people see you growing, even in the midst of financial pressures? When one of you is confined to a hospital bed, what does it show to have the other person at the bedside day after day?

Sadly, Christians today are statistically as likely to head to divorce as those who are not Christians. All marriages face the same basic issues.

But the good news is that Christian marriages have the power and the resources to work through their issues and grow closer together and closer to God in the middle of all the junk and funk they may face. Your marriage might be the only mirror available for your neighbors to see Jesus Christ. What image are they seeing?

As Christ-followers, we're called to be salt and light to the world. Nowhere is that more needed than in marriage relationships. People are crying out for role models in marriage. Be that role model to a watching world.

Marriage is for You

Let me appeal to your selfish nature for a minute. When you stay married through thick and thin, everybody wins. Your spouse, your children and the world that is watching all catch glimpses of God's character and nature. But you win too.

Think about the character that you will develop in marriage. When you say "I do" you may not realize that you are signing up for a lifetime of character school. The good and the bad thing is that we never fully graduate.

Discipline

For example, think about discipline. Where do you really develop discipline? Do you get it while working out and pumping iron? Do you develop discipline by running four or five times a week? Doing pilates? Power walking? Those are great examples of physical discipline.

Real discipline, though, the kind of discipline that builds you on the inside and out, is developed on the rugged plains of marital reality. What is discipline? Discipline is doing what you ought to do so you can then do what you want to do. If you stay married during the easy and the difficult times, you develop the kind of discipline that God's wants you to have. And through discipline, going through the tough stuff, you'll be able to experience all that you want to in your marriage.

Endurance

Endurance is another huge character quality that is developed through marriage. It's more than that cardiovascular benefit that allows you to run two miles instead of one. Endurance is crashing through quitting points.

You are going to face those quitting points in marriage, there's no doubt about it. Anyone who is married has them. You have them in year one and you have them in year twenty-one.

Where is endurance built? Where do we get the lasting benefits of endurance? Not on a track, not at the health club. We get the benefits of endurance in our marriage. And as you crash through those quitting points, God will allow us to breakthrough to a new level in marriage and in life.

Vision

What about vision? That seems like an odd quality for marriage. But it's essential if you're going to get the most out of life. You don't get vision from a leadership book. It's not an idea born from Bill Gates or Bono. Real vision is seeing the unseen.

If you want to develop your ability to see the unseen, resolve to just stay married. Because as you do, you'll begin to see what God sees. As you build discipline and endurance, you will start to see your marriage the way God sees it. You will start to see new solutions to old problems. Once you and your spouse get God's vision for your marriage, He will help you start to move in concert together as one.

Creativity

Each and every one of us is made in the image of our creative Creator. God is a creative genius; so that means you are a creative genius. You don't have to take an art class to develop creativity. You don't have to learn to play the guitar in order to discover your creativity. You're already creative.

Your husband is a creative genius. Your wife is a creative genius. You are a creative genius. And there is no better place for creativity to be lived out than in your marriage.

Marriage is about romance. And romance is all about creativity. It is being predictably unpredictable in the way you love and care for your spouse. Surprise him with a new outfit. Surprise her with a dynamic date. Confuse your spouse (in a good way) by breaking out of what is expected and doing something totally unexpected. Watch the excitement that is infused into your marriage because of this unbelievable trait called creativity. Creativity breeds change and change breeds growth.

Marriage is a 24/7 character school and you only reap the amazing benefits when you stay married. If you're moving from relationship to relationship, you're cheating yourself from developing amazing, God-honoring character. You'll never discover who God wants you to be. You'll never stand out from the crowd.

In the end, God said it best: *For this reason, make every effort to add to your faith goodness to goodness, knowledge; and to knowledge, self-control; and to self-control, perseverance; and to perseverance, godliness; and to godliness, brotherly kindness; and to brotherly kindness, love.*[5]

Guess what? There's no better place than marriage for a crash course to develop these amazing character qualities.

Marriage is about the gospel. And the gospel is about marriage. The math of marriage is $1 + 1 = 1$. That oneness is wholeness when we stick it out together. It is the mirror where Jesus is seen clearly. It is the avenue where your spouse, your kids and the world see the implications of the gospel in our world today. Finally, it is for you.

If you go back and look at those three (Jesus, Others, You), it spells JOY. Because a marriage done God's way is not about happiness; it's about joy: that supernatural quality that rises above our circumstances and transcends fleeting feelings. And in the end, we all crave a marriage that has the ability to soar above the superfluous along the rugged plains of marital reality

A TIME FOR REFLECTION

James 1:23-24

Anyone who listens to the word but does not do what it says is like a man who looks at his face in a mirror and, after looking at himself, goes away and immediately forgets what he looks like.

Questions:

When your children look at your marriage, how do they experience security and strength in their own lives?

What is one thing you can do today to show your spouse that you are thinking more about their needs than your own?

_____
_____
_____
_____
_____
_____
_____
_____
_____
_____
_____
_____
_____
_____
_____
_____
_____
_____
_____
_____
_____
_____
_____
_____
_____

_____

_____

_____

_____

_____

_____

_____

_____

_____

_____

_____

_____

_____

_____

_____

_____

_____

_____

_____

_____

_____

_____

_____

_____

_____

CHAPTER 3

TAMING THE NOSE HAIRS

"I want to wait until I'm 100% sure."

"I'm going to work on my career first."

"I'm holding out for Angelia Jolie."

"When I get my house and sports car, then I'll worry about getting married."

"When I finish backpacking through Europe, then I'll settle down."

SOUND FAMILIAR? Those are just some of the excuses many single adults, particularly men, make for not stepping over the line of marital commitment. For many, marriage has lost its appeal. Exchanging vows has been replaced by making excuses. Why is that? Why has it become so difficult for people today to get married and stay married?

Marriage is a mirror that reflects the nature and character of God. It reflects the sacrificial love of our Creator. And the best marriages are those which showcase the power of the death, burial and resurrection of Jesus Christ.

Because of that, marriage is for you; but not only you. In the previous chapter, we saw how marriage is about JOY—Jesus, Others and You. We spent some time talking about the reasons we should focus on others as we process the "I do's" from our wedding ceremonies.

In this chapter, I want to appeal to your selfish side. Let's face it, we like to think about ourselves, what makes us look good and makes us feel good. It's the "me, myself and I" mentality that we're all familiar with. So for the next few pages, I want to look at what marriage does for *you*. Because whether you are already married or thinking about marriage, it's good to talk about the personal benefits of this union between a man and a woman.

Our culture is becoming increasingly skeptical about marriage. For many of us, marriage has become a burden rather than a blessing. It's an albatross rather than one of our greatest assets. Why?

Maybe we look back to our own childhood at a broken family and we're afraid we'll end up like our parents.

Maybe we look around at our friends who are married and unhappy and we refuse to sign up for anything like that.

Or maybe we are just simply commitment-phobic. We're putting marriage off as long as we can, afraid to commit now because "someone better might come along."

I love talking to single guys. I've talked to a lot of single guys in their 20s, 30s and 40s who tell me the same things about marriage. But truly, when it comes to talking about marriage, single guys are clueless about the benefits of marriage. And I think that cluelessness has them scared to death of marriage.

Recently I did a talk with the single guys as my laser target. I called it, "Just Get Married." And I was talking primarily to the guys who are committed Christians. A lot of those Christian single guys will come up with any number of excuses to explain why they want to wait to get married. One man told me that he wanted to travel more before he "settled down;" he wanted to make sure he had seen more of the world before he committed himself to a woman. Yet, this guy had traveled all around the USA, Europe and had even gone to Australia. Maybe he thought a wife would slow him down. Or maybe he was hung up on the romantic notion that he would fall madly in love with a gorgeous woman with a sexy accent. I'm not sure. But I do know that it was an excuse he was using to cover up his fear of commitment. Did I mention that this guy was in his mid-30s? I wasn't talking to a 22 year old guy who had just graduated from college.

Another guy recently told me that he wanted to make more money first. He said that he wanted to really establish himself in his career, build a house, buy a car and *then* walk down the wedding runner. He wanted to accomplish his version of the American dream and then add a wife to the mix. But it never occurred to him that those are all things a husband and wife should experience together as God-given companions. This was another guy who was well into his 30s and was still waiting to get married.

One of the most popular objections I've heard is, "Ed, I want to wait until I'm 100% sure before I get married. I want to make sure that no one better comes along, because I'll never forgive myself if I let the perfect girl get away."

I almost die laughing when I hear this one. It would be rude to outright laugh in their face, but that's got to be one of the dumbest things I hear over and over again for why singles do not get married.

Are you joking? If we were 100% sure, there would be no reason for the quality that God rewards most: faith.

Certainty, 100% certainty, is not going to happen. In fact, I would say that if you are 100% certain, something is wrong. Go through a year or two with your boyfriend or girlfriend and some healthy doubts will begin to surface. After you make it through the infatuation cycle, your relationship will encounter some bumps in the road and you'll have to decide how much you really love the other person. But don't enter a relationship thinking you have to be completely sure. And don't string along your girlfriend or boyfriend for years and years as you wait for certainty to surface, because it ain't gonna happen!

I wasn't 100% sure when I got engaged to Lisa. And as I said earlier, I didn't really know what I was signing up for when I said, "I do" in a rented tux in front of God and those witnesses over twenty-six years ago. Ignorance truly is bliss sometimes.

Too many guys are waiting to just get married. They are afraid of cashing in their chips too soon, because that better looking, smarter or more cultured woman might just come along. They truly believe that marriage is the last step in their development. They wait until the last possible moment: until their waist size has expanded from a 31 to a 36; their hair has fallen out; and their energy level has waned. And then they wonder why they can't find a Christian version of Angelina Jolie! Guys, take a look in the mirror (read: reality check) before you hold out for a woman with the character of Mother Theresa and the curves of Pamela Anderson.

I'm not trying to beat up the single guys, but I've listened—and watched—too many of them make excuses that lead to relational mistakes. It's also just the opposite of what the Scriptures tell us. The Bible says that if you are a full-court follower of Christ with the desire for the opposite sex, you should just get married. To say it another way: If you love God and love women, just get married. Ladies, if you love God and love men, just get married.

Marriage is assumed throughout Scripture. Did you know there is no word for "bachelor" in the Old Testament? You aren't going to find it. From Genesis to Revelation, marriage is the standard for human beings. There are very, very few situations where singleness is desirable over marriage. The most blatant exception is the Apostle Paul. If you really feel God calling you to be single, pursue that path. But for most of us, marriage is the norm.

For the majority of people following Christ, marriage is not only the best choice, but also it's the only choice. And if you put it off too long, you will be missing out on some of the greatest gifts of marriage. For the vast majority of people, I could easily make the argument that the longer you put off marriage, the longer you are missing God's will for your life. That's a bold statement, but I'll unpack it.

God is pro-marriage. It was His invention within the first few chapters of the Bible. And God modeled the genius of marriage by making it the only human relationship that is analogous to His special relationship to His people.

And immediately after God created man and woman, He said to them, "Be fruitful and multiply."[1]

He wasn't talking about mathematics; He was talking about the beauty and wonder of sexual intimacy in marriage. Throughout Scripture, marriage was seen as one of God's greatest gifts for a man and woman. Marriage produced children. And children produced nations. With very, very few exceptions, marriage was the normal experience for a single man and single woman throughout the Bible. I'm talking about biblical greats like Adam, Abraham, Esther, Ruth,

David and Peter—they all enjoyed the holy union of marriage.

But we've made marriage too complex. We've constructed too many man-made obstacles to getting married. In the minds of many singles, marriage has become something that mere mortals cannot possibly achieve because of the battery of tests and surveys—just to see if we qualify. That's not to say that there isn't wisdom in pre-marital counseling. I strongly recommend that couples spend a minimum of one year together, going through all the seasons, and that they seek pre-marital counseling before getting married. In fact, our church requires it for couples who are married by one of our pastors.

At its base, though, marriage is simply one man and one woman together in covenant. And the longer you wait to get married, the harder it will be to take the plunge.

Do you remember the high dive when you were a kid? The longer you felt the breeze at the top of the diving board, the harder it was to jump into the pool below. Doubt crept in and made a home in your mind. Fear set in. And soon, you were frozen on the stairs while the other kids passed you by to take their turn.

We have muddied God's view of marriage by creating even more barriers to our already skeptical view of this covenant. I think it would help to get back to the benefits of marriage and see how this union is made to give us the most in life and help us in ways we may not have realized before. Let me give you just three compelling reasons why marriage is not only good, but great.

sex

Just seeing that word on the page probably got your attention. But that three letter word is more than something that grabs our attention every time we see it. It's one of the reasons marriage is beneficial for you. It's a small word that helps solve some of our biggest challenges in life.

First and foremost, it solves the problem of sexual temptation. Men and women are sexual creatures. We are wired for sexual desire. In the past, we were told and taught that sexual desire was almost exclusively a man thing; that sex was something that was at the forefront of his mind. But it's not just men anymore. Increasingly, we are discovering that sex is very important for women as well.

Whether you are a man or a woman, if you have the desire for the opposite sex, it's a good thing because it's a God thing. Sex isn't something that we're supposed to run from or not discuss or pretend doesn't exist. God intends for us to experience all the joys and benefits of sex. But here's the caveat: If we're going to get the most out of sex, we're to practice it within the confines of the marital covenant. Like my snorkeling experience in the Caribbean, we are to enjoy this amazing gift of sex within the reef of protection in marriage.

Think of sex like a Ferrari. The Ferrari is one of the most amazing cars that has ever been engineered. It is beautiful to look at, with its unique lines, winged doors and vibrant colors. It's also one of the most impressive cars from a technical standpoint. It has been designed and engineered to do some phenomenal things on the open road.

What if someone were to hand you the keys to a brand new Ferrari? I'm talking about a once-in-a-lifetime opportunity to drive one of the finest cars on the road today. What would you do with this dream car? Would you trash it? Would you take it off-roading into some jagged forest or drive it on some pothole-infested, gravel road? No! A Ferrari is meant for the open road.

You take care of a Ferrari. You buff it, wax it and protect it. It is meant for the Autobahn. That is what a Ferrari is for.

In the same way, we have been given the keys to this amazing gift called sex. But so many people trash it, abuse it and misuse it. They take this gift that has been divinely engineered for marriage and relegate it to the trash heap of society, assuming it's for anyone, anywhere, anytime.

Let me remind you of what God said in Genesis. *For this reason a man will leave his father and mother and be united to his wife, and they will become one flesh.*[2]

The difficult part of marriage is that little word, "become." Yes, we can get married. We can have sex. We can share a bank account. But becoming one flesh? That's the tough part. That's the supernatural part. That's the part that takes me out of the equation and instead forces me to focus on my spouse's needs first.

The math in marriage is $1 + 1 = 1$. Oneness in marriage is two fallen and fallible people becoming mysteriously and wonderfully one. It's two self-centered sinners become one. And when you have sexual intercourse between a husband and a wife, you have the closest experience to true intimacy a human being can ever have this side of eternity. In sexual intercourse between a husband and wife, the nature and character of God are reflected. You have the feminine aspects joining together with the masculine aspects. You also have a reflection of the mysterious oneness of the Trinity—God the Father, God the Son, God the Holy Spirit; three in one, one in three.

If you are single and you have a passion for the opposite sex, *It is better to marry than to burn with sexual desire.*[3] If you have that desire, God's will for you is to get married. And the great news is that when you do get married, your sex life with your spouse will cause you to seek God in a deeper and more passionate way. Let that statement sink for a minute.

Do not deprive each other unless perhaps by mutual consent and for a time, so that you may devote yourself to prayer.[4]

When we look at this directive in Scripture, a few things come to light. First, it is okay to abstain from sex in marriage, for a brief period of time. Because when a man and wife agree to abstain for the purposes of prayer, they can express a more concerted effort to understand God's will. But there's another valid application here.

A prolonged abstinence from sex between a husband and wife can actually distract us in our relationship with God.

When a man and woman get married and, for lack of a better word, exercise their sexual nature, it becomes like an appetite. And when sex is removed from the equation, it can lead to frustration and hurt feelings. Those feelings can easily become a distraction for the wife or the husband—distraction in their relationship; distraction in their daily lives; distraction in their spiritual lives.

According to Paul, spouses have to be careful that they do not deprive the other one of their sexuality. He makes the argument in Scripture that a husband's body belongs to the wife; and the wife's body belongs to the husband.[5]

When you make love to your spouse, your mind and will are more open to be devoted to the Lord. Christians actually serve one another and draw closer to God when they exercise their sexuality in marriage.

Those who misunderstand and abuse the gift of sex say, "I don't want to get married because I don't want to be with the same person for the rest of my life."

But when someone pursues sex outside of marriage, whether it is pre-marital sex or extra-marital sex, that person is harming their body and weakening their influence for Christ. And the "freedom" that they wanted to experience actually becomes a prison of a mis-used gift.

Our culture has trashed the gift of sex and traded its beauty for a series of images or simply an exchange of pleasure. Casual and un-committed sex is the kind of sex that is glamorized in Hollywood, but also the kind of sex that leads to all sorts of spiritual, emotional and physical issues.

As I said earlier, marriage is a mirror that reflects the depth and richness of God. Marriage reflects the unity of God; the myste-rious and holy oneness that is found in the Trinity. It is a covenant that establishes security and allows us to express ourselves fully in the arms of our beloved. When believers are married and express themselves sexually in the confines of the marital bed, they are fully alive and able to relate to God as holy, whole beings.

When we choose to express ourselves sexually outside the marriage bed, we trade our wholeness for fractions. We give our whole selves away to partner after partner; trading and devaluing our humanity, giving more and more of ourselves away with each sexual escapade.

If you have been sexually active and are not married; or if you are thinking about it, let me encourage you. God can restore you from any sin. So starting today, I urge you to preserve your whole self until you pledge yourself to the one person God has for you—your spouse. Because when you experience sex within the covenant of marriage, you'll be experiencing one of the greatest benefits of marriage.

SLOTHS

Sloths are tree-dwelling creatures that pretty much lie around and do nothing. They are slimy, grimy and to be quite frank, a little bit gross looking. When I think about sloths, I think about guys.

Guys are basically lazy. Not many women struggle with this particular vice, but I know a lot of guys are this way. If we had our choice, we'd lie around on the couch and watch TV, not doing much of anything. Too many guys are just hanging out until something on *ESPN* catches our attention. "Oh man, did you see that dunk? Wow! That was an incredible catch! That was phenomenal!"

Guys have this tendency to laze around, staying void of commitment and ingenuity in their lives. They are content to be spectators in the game of life rather than activators who use their God-given gifts and God-driven creativity to spread the light of Christ to the watching world. One of the benefits of marriage is getting you off the couch and into the game, because marriage can cure slothfulness.

It takes work to get a business off the ground. It takes work to be creative. It takes work to take an idea and carry it through to completion. It even takes work to design and produce the electronic devices that turn many people into zombies.

But so many times, we don't want to work. We don't want to try. We don't want to take initiative. We're just sloths.

Singles guys, the longer they balk at marriage, have this gravitational pull toward weirdness. For some reason, guys (especially singles) have the innate ability to isolate themselves from relationships. But the more they isolate themselves, the weirder they get. They start to lose track of reality. And before you know it, you'll be a single guy stammering and staggering your way through an awkward conversation in a social setting because you can't relate. Your fashion will even start to suffer!

Guys, we need women to keep us from getting weird. We need women to help us with our fashion, to show us that our white tube socks don't match our dark suit pants. We need the polite correction when she sees that our nostril hair is long enough to braid. We need women to help us navigate the conversations at a dinner party. We need women to keep us from being the sloth on the couch!

And once you get married, you can't be a sloth anymore. When a single guy gets married, an amazing transformation occurs, much like a caterpillar turning into a beautiful butterfly.

As iron sharpens iron, so one person sharpens another.[6]

Whether you are married or single, the covenant of marriage is one of the best places to exercise your God-given ingenuity. It's where you can stop your laziness and get rid of your, I'll-do-it-tomorrow mentality. In marriage, you'll begin to use your initiative to be romantic, dynamic and full of creativity. And as you commit yourself to doing the work of "becoming" one with your spouse, you'll discover the benefit of marriage curing your slothfulness.

God has created us in His image. And it took work. God walked into the scene of Scripture creating the universe we know today.

In the beginning God created....[7]

At the end of Scripture, we see God continuing to do the work of creating.

I am making everything new.[8]

And because we are made in His image, we are creative geniuses. There is no better place to exercise our God-driven creativity than in the marriage covenant. We shouldn't squeeze out all our creativity in business or the education field. Marriage is the one place we should strive to work and create, because it is the one place we can truly reflect all that God wants us to reflect to the watching world.

It's time to step up and to step out and do the work that God has created you to do. And if you identify with that sloth, it's time to crawl off the couch and get into the game of life that is going on around you. And marriage is the best place for that to happen.

Spiritual Maturity

God has always been, and will always be, completely whole and lacking nothing. So when He created mankind, it wasn't because He needed human beings to make Himself feel more secure or happier. He didn't need us to worship Him to help build His self-esteem. He created us simply out of love—complete, sacrificial, whole love.

Jesus was the promised Messiah who came to deliver the nation of Israel and ultimately humanity from sin. He knew that His own people would reject Him, humiliate Him and hand Him over for crucifixion. But did He waver from His course? No. Jesus continually focused on others; specifically the marginalized, the lame and the sick.

John 3:16 is one of the most popular verses in the Bible. You have seen it at the Super Bowl and emblazoned on church marquees. And no other verse captures the reality of God's love in action.

For God so loved the world that He gave His one and only Son, that whoever believes in Him shall not perish but have eternal life.

Jesus didn't pray for someone else to carry out God's will for His life. He didn't fast and wait for another answer from God. He didn't write a love letter and leave it on a tree for us to find. He gave His life. God's love was and is a sacrificial love.

Marriage is the same way. It requires sacrifice, selflessness and surrender. Marriage is all about spiritual maturity.

Spiritual maturity isn't a selfish endeavor. It's others-driven. When we get married, we are forced to deal with our baggage and junk from the past if we want to have any hope of having a successful future with our spouse. In marriage, we are forced to look into the mirror to discover and deal with our selfishness.

As soon as you get married, you are forced to think about your spouse in several ways. One of those is financially. You have to pause before you buy a new fishing rod or book your next fishing trip. (That isn't theoretical; it is my own burden to bear!)

When you say "I do" you have to think about where you leave your clothes and your dishes—do you pick up after yourself or let him do it?

You have to think about your spouse when your baby deposits another gift in his diaper—do you change it or leave it for her?

You have to think about your spouse when you are in a bad mood—do you withdraw from conversation or share with him what's going on?

You especially have to think about your spouse when you are making love—do you give according to her sexual needs and desires or yours?

Marriage is a 24/7 situation where you are forced outside of your own perspective to think about your spouse. The more you do that, the better your marriage will go. The more time, money and energy you spend on yourself, the worse your marriage will go.

Many people have this misconceived notion of expecting a custom-built bride (or groom) when they head off for their honeymoon. We assume that our spouse will perfectly meet every one of our needs. We assume that things will "just happen" without much thought or energy on our part. That is not reality.

God often uses our own imperfections to sharpen us and our spouse in this beautiful relationship called marriage. That's what it means to see the best and worst of yourself in your spouse. As you look into the marriage mirror, your imperfections will show. And it's during those times that you have the perfect opportunity to grow and mature and change into the person God wants you to become.

If you want to discover what it means to think and act like Christ, you don't have to attend hundreds of Bible studies or fly to some far-off mission field. If you want to really grow in your relationship with God, get married. If you are already married, stay married. One of the greatest things you can do on this side of eternity is to select a godly spouse and allow your marriage to be a witness to the power of the gospel. Work on your marriage so that the world and your family will see Jesus Christ in the mirror of your marriage.

I've grown more spiritually through my marriage than in any other way. Everyday, when I look in the mirror, I constantly see my own selfishness. But marriage has forced me to think about serving Lisa. It has caused me to think less about me and more about what I can do for her. It has helped me to grow spiritually in ways that nothing else has. And that is one of the greatest benefits I will ever experience through my marriage.

You might be thinking, "I can achieve all of that without getting married. I can just live with someone and not have to hassle with the whole marriage thing." Let me rant a little here, because that kind of thinking is totally whack. I'm tired of what the world is telling us about sex and marriage. I'm tired of the constant message to just "hook up with someone; play house with someone." That's totally abusing the beauty and the holiness of the marriage covenant. And it's destroying the legacy that God wants to build through us. I'll talk more about that in a subsequent chapter. But the bottom line is: playing house is not marriage. That kind of relationship will not take you to the next level of sexual fulfillment, of selflessness or spiritual maturity. It just won't.

I've been a pastor for a long, long time. I have preached numerous times a weekend for the last twenty years, in addition to countless seminars, conferences and dialogues with various people. That's a lot of talking. You want to know a secret? In all that time and through all those conversations, I've realized one thing. The greatest sermon I will ever preach is not what I say behind a pulpit or on some stage. The greatest sermon I will ever preach is the reflection I give to my spouse, my kids and the world through my marriage.

When I get outside of my selfishness and serve Lisa, I have the opportunity to build supernatural security and love into her life. When my kids watch me decrease so that my marriage can increase, not only do I experience incredible benefits, but also my family does. When I stick through the storms of life with Lisa, the world sees forgiveness, endurance and most importantly, the gospel.

I don't always feel like it; I don't always wake up wanting to work on my marriage. But I know God will continue to use my marriage as the greatest opportunity to reflect the nature and character of Him this side of eternity.

Marriage doesn't solve everything, but it has done phenomenal things in my life. And it can do the same for you as you commit to the covenant of marriage.

A TIME FOR REFLECTION

1 CORINTHIANS 7:3-4

The husband should fulfill his marital duty to his wife, and likewise the wife to her husband. The wife's body does not belong to her alone but also to her husband. In the same way, the husband's body does not belong to him alone but also to his wife.

QUESTIONS:

How can you use the gift of sex in your marriage to grow you closer as a couple and closer to God?

In what ways is your marriage a venue for you to be spiritually challenged, strengthened and matured?

CHAPTER 4

CUDDLING ON THE COUCH?

MARRIAGE IS PHENOMENAL. The ability to be totally intimate with another person—spiritually, emotionally and sexually—is the closest we can be to anyone on this side of eternity. The opportunity to share life with your best friend makes it easier. Marriage makes the highs higher and makes the lows more bearable. But a great marriage isn't automatic.

Marriage is not the easiest thing; so often it is the hardest thing. But it can become the greatest thing when you're willing to do it God's way.

Marriage is not about euphoric feelings; it's not about the often elusive quality called "happiness." Yes, there are many moments of happiness in marriage, but there's much more involved. Marriage is a covenant between a husband and wife before God.

Sadly, though, our culture has decaffeinated marriage, and we misunderstand what it really is and what it really takes. We see celebrities walk down the wedding runner for a quick photo-op and then run to the nearest courthouse to sever the tie. And many people see that and think they'll enter marriage because there's always an easy out.

Other people get married for the tax break or because they have exhausted all other options and it's the last thing to cross off their to-do list. When you compare the flippant manner with which so many people treat marriage and divorce, it is sad.

Culture teaches us that marriage is merely a transaction between people. That line of thinking shows that most of us don't know the depth, the richness and the beauty of a biblical marriage. And it shows that we enter into marriage with the wrong mindset.

Because we can have a false understanding of what marriage is, we can walk down the aisle with a false understanding of what it will take.

Over the next few pages, let me share what Lisa and I have learned as we have processed our own marriage and as we've studied the Scriptures about this beautiful, yet often mysterious relationship between a man and a woman. We've found out over the years that there is one thing that separates the great marriages from the not-so-great marriages. The secret is revealed in one four letter word. No, I'm not talking about that choice word you want to unleash on your spouse in the middle of an argument. I'm talking about another four letter word: *work*.

DON'T JUST GET MARRIED…UNLESS

I hope you didn't run out and get married after reading the previous chapter. Because while there are a lot of amazing things that happen when we commit to our spouse before God and those we love, none of them will happen if you are not willing to put forth the effort that marriage requires. So save yourself the trouble. Because if you get married without realizing what I'm getting ready to unpack, you will not only mess up your own life; but also you'll mess up the other person's life. And if you happen to have children and then decide that this marriage thing isn't what you thought it was, you'll mess up their lives too. So don't enter into the covenant of marriage with the wrong mindset or without understanding the work involved.

As a pastor I've heard a lot of funny things about marriage, a lot of misconceptions and misconceived ideas. I don't want to pick on the singles in my church too much, but here are a few more classics I've heard unmarried people tell me concerning their ideas of marriage.

Some tell me that they can't wait to sit in front of the fire with their new husband and talk for hours on end. One single guy recently told me, in the middle of a meeting, that he looks forward to the day when he will spend his nights cuddling on the couch with his wife. I had to laugh. Because while there are certainly moments when those romantic, intimate encounters happen in marriage, it takes a lot more than plopping down on the couch in front of a fire to make it work.

To make a marriage work, you've got to be willing to do the work. Many couples feel like saying, "I don't," only months after pledging, "I do," because that's when the honeymoon is over and reality begins. And they don't realize the fact that this relationship is going to take some serious effort on their part.

So before you start lighting the candles and reaching for your Barry White playlist, you better be willing to put in the work to set the table for such moments.

Another person told me, "I think I'm going to get married, because it will simplify everything."

I had a very hard time keeping a straight face when I heard that. What? Marriage will simplify your life? I'd like to meet the married couple who thinks their lives are simpler now that they are married! And if you add kids into the mix…somebody needs a reality check!

Listen to what the Apostle Paul says, *Whatever you do work at it with all of your heart as you're working for the Lord, not for men.*[1]

Notice that word, "Whatever." That means if you are an employee, work at it with all your might. If you are a student, study with all your energy. And if you are married, work at your marriage with everything you have.

Simply put, marriage equals work.

When you understand that fact, it can revolutionize the way you think about marriage, whether you are already married or have marriage on your radar screen. And if that's you, if you have that desire to get married, make sure you are willing to work at it with all of your heart. As you visualize long walks and late dinners over candlelight, spend as much time visualizing yourself serving your spouse when she's mad at you. Visualize asking for forgiveness even though you know that he's the one who was 95% wrong. Ultimately, you are not just working for your marriage; you are working for the Lord when you say, "I do."

Let's unpack this thing called work, because if we don't understand work, we'll never understand marriage.

Work is Worship

Worship is a celebration; it is responding with passion to a person or event. We all worship. And many times we don't even realize it.

You can go to any big name concert and see 20,000 people

swaying back and forth to the music. That's worship.

Turn on the TV and watch late night commercials play to our worship of self. It doesn't matter if it's a real estate seminar or the latest fitness machine; we know how to motivate others to lust after more money or a better body.

In America, we worship the NFL. It doesn't matter if it's the middle of October or the middle of March; it's all football all the time on the radio and around the water cooler.

NASCAR is another place of worship for thousands and thousands of people who pack into racetracks of exhaust, neon signs and lots of adult beverages. There is some serious worship happening at these tracks. People worship NASCAR.

All of these situations are great examples of passionate intensity and strong worship. But they all have the wrong object. Everybody knows how to worship whether it's our bodies, our bank account, our sports team or our favorite singers. We worship all the time because we are wired by God for worship.

As a believer, everything I do should be an act of worship—to God. And marriage is one of the greatest places where true worship can happen.

In the covenant of marriage, I'm supposed to reflect the love and the grace of Jesus Christ as I work for my spouse. And as I serve, as I forgive, as I speak kindly to my wife when I'm angry, I'm worshipping Christ.

Real worship isn't just singing songs and holding up our hands in church. It's not merely listening to some preacher or reciting the ancient creeds.

Present your body as a living sacrifice; holy, acceptable to the Lord. This is your spiritual act of worship.[2]

When I give my whole life to God, that's worship. This means

I give Him my finances, my dreams, my career, my comfort, even my marriage.

And when Lisa and I commit to working for and on our marriage, we are also worshipping. When I give myself fully to Lisa and she gives herself fully to me, it isn't just a physical thing. It's not just a financial thing or an emotional thing. And it's not just something that happens on our good days. We've got to give each other our all—the good, the bad and the ugly.

None of us can hope to compartmentalize our lives spiritually, emotionally, physically or intellectually. We can't divide our worship between different aspects of life. We have to worship with all we are and have and do, including and especially in our marital relationship. But in order for this to happen, we can't expect to do it on our own.

A vibrant and whole marriage is fueled by God. It is the man dying to himself in order to live for God and for his wife. It is the wife dying to her needs and desires in order to serve God and her husband.

What are people learning about God by the way you are treating your husband? Are they seeing unconditional love and unmerited grace? When your golf buddies eavesdrop on a cell phone conversation between you and your wife, what are you teaching them about the kindness and others-first character of God? Are you building her up in front of your friends rather than tearing her down?

We have to hold marriage to a holy standard because God is holy. The marital covenant is the only human relationship that mirrors God's relationship to His Church. And if we are going to worship Him, our marriage needs to reflect that.

Once we bow the knee to Jesus, once we've said "I do" to Him, we have responded to Him in worship. Going back to the verse that

Paul penned in Colossians 3, everything we do, say, touch, taste and feel should be an act of worship to the Lord Himself.

So as you think about worship, begin to think about your marriage as a platform to exercise your worship. I'm not talking about worshipping your husband or making a shrine for your wife; I'm talking about loving and serving them as an act of worship to Jesus Christ, the lover of your soul.

As I said earlier, the greatest sermon I will ever preach is not from some platform in church. It is not some leadership lesson I will share with Christian leaders from around the world. The greatest sermon I will ever preach is the way I treat Lisa. If I speak eloquently to the church, but speak harshly to my best friend, I have invalidated the Word of God in my own life.

The same is true in your marriage. You may not be a pastor, but you are a witness for the gospel through your marriage. And if you are constantly ignoring your husband's needs, a two-hour quiet time reading the Bible won't do much good for your marriage. If you are damaging your wife with the words you speak, the words you communicate with God won't go very far. The Bible is primarily for our application, not our information. So put the work into your marriage that the Bible talks about. And discover how your marriage can become a place of worship to the Lord.

WORK IS ORDER

Work is about worship, but work is also about order. God is the God of order. Everything He does, has done or will ever do emerges out of His perfect order and structure.

If you ever feel like you're out of order; if you ever feel disjointed; if you ever find yourself asking why you feel disconnected or like things just aren't clicking, you are out of God's order.

God has laid His plans for us throughout Scripture. There is freedom to live when we stay within the confines of God's order, but there is chaos and destruction waiting for us when we venture outside the reef of a covenant marriage, outside of the order God has set forth.

A perfect example is sex. We don't make the rules for sex, God does. He tells us that sex is reserved for one man and one woman within the protection and provision of marriage. He doesn't make those stipulations to rain on our sexual parade. It's all about His order.

Marriage isn't some fluid thing that we get to change with the cultural tide. Satan, though, the enemy of God, is very crafty. And he wants us to think that God's order is outdated or irrelevant in today's culture. When you think about Satan, don't think of a red suit and a pitchfork. Don't think about some sulfur-breathing dragon. He's more real, and much more sinister than that.

What the devil tries his best to do is subtly twist God's perfect design for something and pervert it. And he's done his best to pervert God's design for sex.

Our bodies are temples for the Holy Spirit. They are beautiful creations from God and we are to take care of them as an act of worship to God.[3] Some people trash their bodies with junk food, or by abusing substances that destroy their God-given designs. Others take the lies of Satan to worship their own body instead of the Creator who made it. Hours and hours are spent everyday consumed by the desire to worship the person in the mirror at the expense of other people, and even God.

Sex is one of the most beautiful gifts we have been given. It is the perfect compliment for the female and the male anatomy. It is the perfect union of the female and the male characteristics of God. Sex is full of pleasure, and sex is also used to build a family. Sex expresses true intimacy better than any other way. And as I said before, it is the best experience that mirrors the oneness of God.

But again, Satan manipulates and perverts sex into simply an exchange of pleasure. Casual sex replaces covenant sex. One night stands replace the oneness that God wants to build into marriages.

Even our culture, which promotes this lower view of sex, knows better. If you read between the lines on sex-crazed sitcoms or blockbuster movies, you see the heartache, loneliness and destruction that this distorted view of sex creates. Ultimately, it leaves single people lonelier and less whole, less human. They end up feeling used rather than loved.

Sex is made for marriage and marriage is made for sex. I'm saddened by the destruction caused by premarital sex. I'm tired of seeing committed Christians fall into the trap of living together, or as I call it, "playing house" with one another. If you're in that situation, you are signing yourself up for all kinds of trouble because you are swimming outside of God's protective reef, outside of His order. And when you do that, all bets are off.

Order is God's established standard for us to live by. When we live our lives based on the cues from Scripture, we discover freedom, success and most importantly, the peace that comes from living in the will of God.

Order, though, is not about our feelings. Feelings can seriously mess us up. Lisa hasn't always felt like denying her own needs to look after mine. I can guarantee that she would rather spend more vacations in the mountains than the many we have spent near water so I could fish.

Feelings are funky. If I based my life on feelings, I would have bolted on my marriage a long time ago. I haven't always felt like loving Lisa as Christ loved the Church. But my life is based on more than feelings; it is based on God's plan, God's design, God's order for my life.

When I talk about order, one of the biggest things we need to understand is that God has created an order for the roles within marriage. As husband and wife, Lisa and I are equal in form but unique in function. In that, we reflect the equality of the Trinity. But we also reflect the diversity of the differing roles within the Trinity.

God has established the leadership in the marriage for the husband.

"Are you saying the man is superior and the woman is inferior?"

No. Again, the husband and wife are equal. We are both created in the image of God.[4] We are both charged with the responsibility of reflecting the light of Jesus Christ in our world. But in marriage, just like in any partnership, there is responsibility and accountability.

Husbands take their cue from Jesus Christ to love their wives as Christ loved the Church.[5] I don't know of anything in life more difficult than that responsibility. Husbands are called to die to themselves so that the wife is loved, secure and able to flourish. Also, the husband is called the head of the home, and the one who ultimately follows the leadership of Jesus Christ.[6]

I tell the husbands in my church to be "umbrella fellas."[7] When husbands embrace their calling, when they fall under the headship of Christ, they can be used to protect their family from the storms of life. We don't lord the authority over our wives; we lovingly lead through sacrificial service. And when we do that, our wives will gladly fall under the umbrella and help us follow Christ's direction for our families, our careers and our future.

I said before that God is the God of order. The creation story is all about order. When we see this story, we see how God ordered the world systematically to provide life and sustain life. So within order, we have creativity. Creativity takes order and it takes work. Creativity is not chaotic; it is purposeful and inspired by God.

God, in Genesis 1:1, started the creativity process. In fact, it's the fifth word in the Bible. *In the beginning God created....*

Creativity is framed in the Scriptures with the first verse in the Bible and the last few verses of the Bible. In Revelation 21:5, God enters and walks through eternity creating things that are new.

Every single day, as I wake up in this holy and ordered union called the marriage covenant, I have a chance to create something. I can create walls in my marriage or I can create community with my wife. I can create problems in my relationship or I can create solutions that lead to greater intimacy. I truly believe that marriage should be the most creative relationship in the universe, because inside marriage, you have order and you have the blessing of God.

What about romance? Romance is not the stuff of fairy tales or magic potions. Romance is work. And it emerges out of creativity, which is built on order.

If you are a husband, let me focus on you specifically here. What you used to get her is what you should use to keep her. Don't hang your dating jersey in the rafters once you say, "I do." Don't retire your creativity when you walk down the wedding runner. Continue to use your God-given creativity to romance your wife. Work to keep your wife in love with the man she married.

Marriage can be monotonous at times. After months or years together, we get familiar with one another. The mystery tends to fade away. But because of this gift called work, husbands and wives can break through the monotony.

When we practice being predictably unpredictable; when we work at our marriage and at romance, we can confuse our spouse—in a good way. Husbands can surprise their wives with a clean house and a five-star dinner. Wives can trade their "not tonight" nightgown for something a little more inviting. We have to continue to break our tendencies to be comfortable, to be predictable in marriage. And we have to work at showing our creativity in order for our marriages to grow.

WORK IS RECONCILIATION

Marriage is spelled w-o-r-k. We've been talking about worship and order. The third aspect is reconciliation, and it's probably the most difficult thing to practice in marriage. And just like worship and order, it's not an option. As a believer in Jesus Christ, we have to be committed to this.

All this is from God, who reconciled us to Himself through Christ and gave us the ministry of reconciliation.[8]

The word reconciled means that our holy God corrected the gap between Himself and people full of sin like you and me. To say it another way, God paved the way to be married to His people. He reestablished the intimate relationship that He shared with Adam and Eve. The Bible says that these two people "walked with God" in the Garden of Eden—before they sinned. That is true intimacy. And God reconciled us to that level of intimacy.

A great marriage is a place where reconciliation happens regularly. If you look at the second part of that verse above, you'll see that those of us who are believers in Christ have been given the ongoing responsibility of reconciliation. We need to reconcile as co-workers, as fathers and sons, as mothers and daughters, as roommates, as neighbors; and most importantly, as husbands and wives.

You show me a couple who has gone through a divorce and I will show you at least one person who has neglected the ministry of reconciliation. Either the husband or the wife has left the process and the result is the death of a marriage.

What is reconciliation? At its base level, it is the gospel. It's the unmerited favor of God to you and me. And because we have been forgiven so much, we should extend that same forgiveness to our spouse. Marriage should be a place of grace, because our marriages are a reflection of God's relationship with us. We should reflect what God has done through the sacrifice of His Son. Reconciliation with God is something we can't earn and certainly don't deserve. Yet, as we allow Jesus to work in His grace and mercy, we can work those powerful realities out in our marriage.

But reconciliation is messy. And it is probably the most difficult part of marriage. You've got a fallen and fallible sinner on one side of the couch; you've got another fallen and fallible sinner on the other side. Without Christ, a husband and a wife reflect selfishness to each other. You both have issues, you have conflicts and you have junk from your past. Because of that, you're going to have fights and arguments and conflicts and disagreements—yes even you, ecstatic, engaged couple!

Knowing that we are pledging ourselves before God in sickness and in health, for better or for worse, we need to have something supernatural on tap to make it last. That something is the power of the resurrection.

Reconciliation has been given to us by God. And it is something that we are to carry on in our marriages. With reconciliation, the Spirit of God works supernaturally through us. Without it, we fail.

In the previous chapter, I beat up the guys with some of my comments. Some of it was hyperbole, but there is something true to the tendency toward slothfulness and isolation (and weirdness) of some guys. Women, it's your turn. You tend to have a little difficulty with this reconciliation deal.

Guys, generally speaking, don't balk at reconciling. Maybe it's because we are used to messing up; maybe it's just because we don't like dissonance. For whatever reason, before men say, "I do," many of them have practiced saying two other powerful words in the mirror and learned to use them often: "I'm sorry."

God has given us this ability to reconcile. The word "husband" is really from two words, "house" and "band." I am to keep the house banded together through the power of God. I am the umbrella fella. And as such, I am to take the initiative to do the work of reconciliation. When Lisa is 99.9 percent wrong and I'm 0.1 percent wrong, I'm to go to her and initiate reconciliation. I don't say, "Lisa, you were 99.9 percent wrong and I'm only 0.1 percent wrong." That's not right. I say, "Lisa, you know what, I was wrong. Will you forgive me?"

Guys don't usually have a problem saying, "Honey, I'm sorry. Will you forgive me?"

If you are a woman, I know what you are thinking. You're thinking, "Of course men are good are saying I'm sorry. They want to get over the conflict so they can get to the make-up sex!"

There might be some truth to that, but it's ultimately a gift from God. Reconciliation is about the cross. It is about the sacrifice of our Savior for our forgiveness. Whether you are a man or a woman, you should quickly reconcile because of what God did for you.

Generally speaking, women struggle more with reconciliation than men do. There's no question that women are smarter than men. But this is where God has leveled the playing field in the area of emotions.

Women are much more in tune with their emotions than men. And those feelings and emotions can sometimes prolong the reconciliation process—and that can spell trouble. That's why women often struggle more when it comes to seeking reconciliation. It's not that they don't want it, but it's more difficult for them to initiate it.

Women, typically, have a harder time saying, "I'm sorry. I was wrong. Will you forgive me?"

A lot of women will say, "I'm just not there yet, honey. I just don't feel ready yet. Just let me have my space." Then, when they feel like it, they'll find their husband and apologize.

That's not the way reconciliation works. Take a look at Jesus. What if He held grudges against us? What if He said, "I'm just going to wait until I feel it"? What if He said to us, "I want you to prove that you're really sorry before I let you off the hook"?

I'm telling you, reconciliation is tough. It separates the great marriages from those that will fail. Every marriage has the same struggles—whether it's between Angelina Jolie and Brad Pitt or John and Jane Q Public. When it comes right down to it, all marital conflict revolves around PMS. I'm talking about power, money and sex. What did you think I was talking about? Dissonance happens because of power, money and sex.

Successful marriages are the ones that negotiate through those issues and do the work of reconciliation. They are the ones that make the most of this gift that God has given us through the Spirit of God.

Are you using that gift? Are you exercising that aspect of work in your marriage?

WORK IS KNOWLEDGE

How do you spell work? Worship. Order. Reconciliation. Finally, work is knowledge.

We need information about what marriage is so we can apply what it does. We need the 4-1-1 on marriage if we're going to make the most of it. That's why God's Word, marriage conferences and books like these are so important for your ongoing enrichment as a couple. None of us have cornered the market on marital bliss. We need to continually learn from one another and work on this beautiful, but mysterious process of "becoming one."

Knowing What Marriage Is

The first thing we need to know is that marriage is a mirror that reflects the gospel and the nature of God to our spouse. It is a covenant that bonds a husband and wife together under God's umbrella for a lifetime. It is an opportunity to showcase the death, the burial and the resurrection of Christ to our spouse, our families and the world watching us. It is not for elusive feelings of happiness; it is for our holiness.

Because marriage is a mirror, we have the opportunity to see our true reflection in our spouse. That means we see our good side and our ugliness reflected back to us. We see our selfishness, anger, pride and a host of other characteristics we'd rather not see on display. And it gives us the opportunity to work on those in order to become the spouse God wants us to be.

Knowing Your Spouse

In marriage, we have the opportunity to truly know someone more closely, more intimately than anywhere else in life. That is absolutely huge for a growing, thriving marriage. We've got to truly know the other person we have dedicated our lives to.

But sometimes, as time wears on, familiarity can set in. And as the saying goes, familiarity breeds contempt.

So we have to know that heading in. And we have to be very careful that we don't get too complacent toward our spouse. And there are a couple of things we can do to make sure that doesn't become the case.

I think one of the greatest things we can do to head off contempt is to express thanksgiving for our spouse. Rather than being complacent with who our spouse is, we need to express thanks to God for the gift of our spouse. And express thanks to him or her.

Tell your husband how thankful you are for the man that he is. Write a letter to your wife to tell her how thankful you are for her grace and for her lifelong partnership with you. Thank them, because there's no other person on the earth that will ever know you as well or that you will know as well as your spouse.

But also, make sure that in knowing your spouse, you know what they want and need. Many times, we try to reflect our own needs back to our spouse. And because of that, we do for them the things we want done for us. And while that works sometimes, more often than not, we have to know our spouse's unique needs and personality in order to reflect the love of God back to them.

Do you know what makes your husband tick? What is it that absolutely does it for your husband? Is it quality time or a clean house?

What about your wife? Do you know how to show love to your wife in a way that meets her needs? Does she need nonsexual touch or does she want heartfelt words of affirmation?

Take the time to study your spouse—and grow with your spouse through the different stages of your relationship. I promise that it will pay off every time.

Without an understanding of your spouse, you may work very hard at your marriage, but the work may not result in any return. In other words, is the work you're putting into your marriage working for your marriage? Or are you spinning the tires without recognizing and knowing what will really reach your spouse? It's all about understanding the person who stood on the other side of the aisle on your wedding day.

The same can be said for a relationship with Jesus.

Knowing Your Savior

Without an understanding of Jesus Christ and the gospel, it is impossible to have an accurate read on a biblical marriage. Our culture doesn't understand marriage because it doesn't understand Jesus. Once someone is ambushed by the grace and mercy of Jesus, only then can they start to reflect those qualities in their marriage.

When I said, "I do" to Jesus, I began to see the world in a different way. I started to see more of my own junk and saw God's irrational love for me. As Christ was worked the gospel into my own life, I've been able to reflect that same gospel to my wife, Lisa. When I'm having a bad day, Lisa reflects hope and grace to me which encourages me and strengthens me. And it does the same for your marriage too.

People are all about respect these days. Have you heard about that? The cry is, "Man, don't disrespect me." I feel like rattling off some Aretha Franklin, but I won't. Respect is definitely a hot button today. It's one of the favorite words of our young people and especially the young entertainers.

The desire for respect is a good thing, but it's really nothing new. I believe it mirrors a feeling we all long for. But when it comes to marriage, we have to be very careful that we don't demand respect; instead, we should give it. If I'm always thinking, "Lisa, respect me. Lisa, serve me. Take care of me," we will have a horrible marriage.

As a Christ-follower, it's not about getting respect. It's about *giving* respect. If anyone deserves respect, it is the Messiah. If anyone deserves to be praised, respected and served, it is Jesus.

When people misunderstood Him, though, did He bolt? Did He abandon ship and look for greener pastures? No. Jesus stuck it out, did the work and instead of demanding respect, He gave it. He gave it to widows and orphans. He gave it to prostitutes. He gave it to people who could never repay Him. And He gave it freely. He put the work in to save the world, and to save you.

Following Jesus is countercultural. It's the salmon swimming upstream. It's going against the crowd. Jesus taught us that the way to greatness is the path of service. Up is down. The last shall be first. To get more, give more away.

The application for marriage is that it will only grow as we think less about our individual needs. It will click when we spend our time thinking about and serving our spouse, rather than dwelling on our own desires.

It's no wonder the world has totally screwed up marriage. How can our culture get a grasp on a gospel-driven marriage if they don't understand the gospel? How can it understand the marriage mirror if it doesn't comprehend biblical servanthood and forgiveness?

In perhaps the greatest verse of the Bible, John said, *For God so loved the world that he gave....*[9]

God didn't wait until He was shown respect. He initiated the greatest act of love by sacrificing His one and only Son so we could be adopted as children of God. Does your marriage reflect that sacrificial love?

We have talked a lot about Genesis 2:24 in the past few chapters. Let me remind you of that simple, little, three-word phrase that is easy to gloss over, but hard to live out. "Become one flesh."

It's easy to have sex. It's easy to sign a lease together and play house. It's a whole new level when you talk about becoming one flesh—spiritually, emotionally, intellectually and physically. It's difficult to truly know your spouse on a level that will bring about the oneness God wants you to have.

Oneness is the math of marriage. Two shall become one. $1 + 1 = 1$. After more than twenty-six years, I'm still working on that little word, "becoming." And if you talked to Lisa, she would say the same thing about herself.

Talking about respect, the Bible says, *Each one of you also must love his wife as he loves himself and the wife must respect her husband.*[10]

Marriage should be a love and respect contest. As we saw earlier, respect is something we have been given by God in the person of Jesus. And respect in your marriage is a result of the work you put into your marriage

Marriage takes w-o-r-k. And the work is worth it, because marriage is the pinnacle of all human relationships. It is the greatest opportunity you will ever have to know and experience the intimacy of God with another human being. The covenant of a Christ-centered marriage is the greatest opportunity for you to grow in your faith.

And when you get right down to it, the work of marriage is fun.

It is an amazing feeling to know that your best friend is in a lifelong partnership to help you, hang out with you and love you as you grow through the decades together. Marriage is an amazing gift from God. Are you making the most of that gift by doing the work?

A TIME FOR REFLECTION

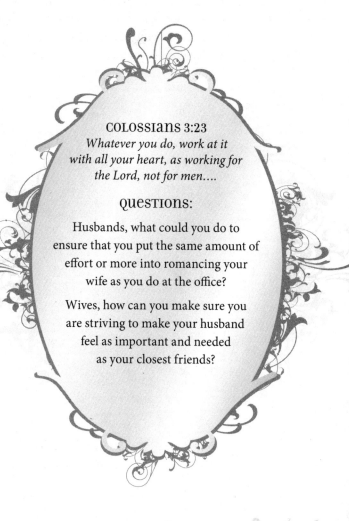

COLOSSIANS 3:23
*Whatever you do, work at it
with all your heart, as working for
the Lord, not for men....*

QUESTIONS:

Husbands, what could you do to
ensure that you put the same amount of
effort or more into romancing your
wife as you do at the office?

Wives, how can you make sure you
are striving to make your husband
feel as important and needed
as your closest friends?

JUST STAY MARRIED

"She's boring me to death."

Just stay married.

"I'm sick of him. Surely there's someone..."

Just stay married.

"I can't stand her anymore. I'm not in..."

Just stay married.

"I never thought I'd say this but I want a..."

Just stay married.

MARRIAGE IS A PARABLE

we've already seen, marriage is an opportunity...
to God and to reflect the gospel in the way...
watching our marriage. But marriage also...

CHAPTER 5

JUST STAY MARRIED

"She's boring me to death."

Just stay married.

"I'm sick of him. Surely there's someone better for me out there."

Just stay married.

"I can't stand her anymore. I'm not happy and I want out."

Just stay married.

"I never thought I'd say this, but I'm ready to move on."

Just stay married.

MARRIAGE IS A GREAT GIFT THAT GOD HAS GIVEN US. As we've already seen, marriage is an opportunity for us to grow closer to God and to reflect the gospel to our spouse and to the world watching our marriage. But marriage isn't easy. Whether you have been married for three days or thirty years, you know that marriage is spelled w-o-r-k. (And if you haven't figured that out yet, go back and re-read the last chapter.)

Marriage is one of the hardest things we'll ever face here on earth. After all, you have two self-centered people trying to do life together, as one. For a marriage to function, those two strong and independent people need to join together for the benefit of the other. It's often a formula for frustration.

But before the book is closed (pardon the pun), let me leave you with some of the reasons why you should just stay married. Because there are some monstrous benefits, if we're willing to do marriage God's way.

There are some benefits from a Christian perspective that I want to address here. And there are some things from a secular perspective as well. Why would I point you outside the Bible after spending the last hundred or so pages pointing you to it? Here's why: I want you to see that the benefits of marriage are pretty much universally valued, whether you open the Bible or not.

GODLY Reasons To Just Stay Married

Evangelism

As I said earlier, the greatest sermon I will ever preach is the way I treat Lisa. The best thing I can do for my kids or anyone else watching is to demonstrate love and affection to Lisa. When I do that, I show everyone that God is active and alive in my marriage.

One of the greatest compliments Lisa and I have ever received happened several months ago. We were out of town, and each day we would walk by a set of shops near the hotel where we were staying. One of those shops was a little jewelry store owned by a Jewish man.

Each day we would walk in, look around and talk with this man. Eventually he found out that I am a pastor. Then, near the end of the week, he stopped us and said, "I want to tell you something. Whatever you're preaching, I know it's real because your marriage is real. You guys truly love each other. I can tell just by the way you treat each other."

When we walked out of the store that day, Lisa and I thought, "Is that incredible?! We're not perfect. But somehow, this man saw God in the way we treat each other. What a compliment!"

I truly believe that we will have the opportunity to lead this gentleman into a relationship with Christ one day. I didn't have to preach a sermon. I didn't say, "Do you have a Bible? Turn to the book of Genesis and let me show you…." I didn't have to do that. He just watched our relationship and saw the love of God through the way we treat each other.

That's the kind of power that we all wield in marriage. That's the kind of power that we leverage to the world watching us. We have the opportunity to showcase the power of our commitment, the power of the marriage mirror.

You know what? There are going to be a lot of holes on the road to holiness in marriage. In our marriage, Lisa and I have hit many, many potholes together. But commitment is where we build the supernatural stuff that catches the attention of a skeptical world.

Hundreds of years ago, St. Francis of Assisi said something very simple, but very profound. He said, "Preach the gospel; use words if necessary."

Our world is highly cynical and critical of churches, pastors and Christianity in general. Most of the time, a sermon isn't what the world needs. You know what it needs? It needs a display of supernatural actions that are contrary to what we, as human beings, can do naturally. The world needs to see marriages that reflect the sacrifice of Christ by a husband who is denying his own needs to serve the needs of his wife; marriages that demonstrate the ability to grow and thrive despite the odds being stacked against them.

And that's one of the greatest benefits of staying married; a phenomenal platform to showcase the good news of Jesus Christ.

Legacy

Legacy is another benefit of staying married. A lot of people talk about this magical word, legacy. I'm glad that people are waking up to the fact that life is short. The author of the book of James tells us that life is a mist, a vapor that appears for a while and then vanishes.[1]

Whether our mist lasts for another five days or fifty years, we better be concerned with what we are leaving behind. We each have the ability to leave a lasting legacy long after we are gone. From the wisdom of bumper stickers and bad pastoral humor, we know that we can't hitch a U-Haul® to a hearse. Your house, car and shoe collection won't make the trip to the other side of eternity with you. So what are you going to leave behind?

One of the most powerful and lasting things you can pass on to future generations is an example of a God-centered marriage. You have the opportunity to build this example into your kids, your church and those outside the family of God. Your marriage might be the only marriage that makes it in your circle of influence. It might be the only marriage that provides a glimpse into the nature and character of God to so many people watching you. And the same goes for me and Lisa.

Years from now, as we look back on life with our spouse, we won't be worried about those petty arguments that every marriage endures. We won't be worried that he left the toilet seat up again or that she ruined our favorite shorts in the laundry. Why? Because those things things aren't involved in building your legacy.

Here's a good exercise for you to do alone or with your spouse: try to remember some of the stupid things that you have fought about in the past. Think back to a time when there was dissonance in your marriage and locate the source of that particular marital spat. If your marriage is anything like ours, you'll laugh at how ridiculous you were to get so worked up over nothing. Most of the time, we can't even remember what we were fighting about.

For a healthy marriage, we need to face our issues head-on and practice reconciliation to grow stronger. As we do, we'll begin to build a legacy, *our* legacy, in the lives of those people around us. And we'll discover another great benefit of marriage.

Security

When you become a believer in Christ, you are permanently adopted into the family of God. It is an eternal arrangement between an all-powerful God and people like you and me. And once you are in God's family, you have a home forever. Our adoption provides incredible security.

And once we have that security, we can begin to live with the kind of offensive energy that God wants us to have. Rather than living defensively, we can begin to take turf for God's kingdom because we realize we aren't fighting *for* victory; we are fighting *from* victory. And our adoption gives us even greater incentives to follow

God's Word. Because we are shown such incredible love from God, we have a sense of security that changes everything.

In your marriage, you have the opportunity to build that same kind of security into your spouse. As you show your spouse that you are in it for the long haul and that you aren't going to bail, you can help them feel secure. Your love will make your husband feel more confident. Your loyalty and faithfulness will make your wife bloom like the rose of Sharon.[2]

I've been saying throughout this book that marriage is a mirror that reflects the nature and character of God. And the eternal security that God has graced us with is one of the most valuable things we can reflect to one another.

Lisa and I have the chance every day to reflect to each other the eternal security that we have in Christ. When you have that kind of security; when you both have resolved to just stay married come hell or high water, you will walk with a spring in your step and lead with a greater sense of power and confidence. And you will live with an agenda that is above and beyond anything this world has to offer. There is nothing like it.

While I've been writing this book, I have had my Bible open on my desk. It's where I base all my teaching and preaching and writing. Any pastor worth his salt will stand on the authority of God's Word. The Bible is our instruction book for life, and in this context, for marriage. Without it, an author has nothing more than a few good ideas that might last a few years—if they're lucky.

But in the last part of this chapter, I want to go secular. I want to look at some benefits of marriage that come from the world of academic researchers and "relational experts." I'm going to tell you what society at-large says about the benefits of marriage. Because while much of our culture may have a whacky and shallow view of marriage, it still understands the truth that marriage has some great benefits. So let's check out what is said about marriage from a secular standpoint.

SECULAR REASONS TO JUST STAY MARRIED

Let me give you a little side bar here before we dive in. What's so hilarious about these next few benefits is the arrogance with which they are communicated to us from the so-called experts of the world today. Whether it is secular psychologists, sociologists, anthropologists or scientists, many of them believe they have discovered something fresh. They truly believe they are telling us something earth-shattering.

But really, these "relationship experts" are re-hashing what the Bible has talked about for thousands of years. It makes me laugh every time I hear one of these people spout off some new benefit of marriage and try to pass it off as new "research." Ok, I got that off my chest. Let's look at some of these benefits.

Life

Number one, if we stay married, we will live longer, more contented lives. According to a recent article in *Time*, single people who never marry are 58% more likely to die sooner than married people.[3]

This same article also explained that married people have lower rates of all types of mental illnesses and suicide. [This study lasted for decades and was consistent across races and income levels.]

This article also quoted the Center for Disease Control and Prevention (CDC) which stated that married people are "less likely to smoke or drink heavily than people who are single, divorced or widowed. These sorts of lifestyle changes are known to lower rates of cardiovascular disease, cancer and respiratory diseases."

Married men seem to receive an even greater benefit from stress relief in marriage. In the journal, *Health Psychology*, men were found to have lower readings of stress hormones when they returned to the refuge of home after a particularly busy day at work.[4]

And a recent university study found that happily married people have lower blood pressure than singles who have a supportive social network.[5]

Let's also consider here the effects of divorce on health and life expectancy. What happens when someone loses their marriage? A study in Denmark found that the death rate among divorced men in their 40s is twice as high as it is for other men in the same age group.[6] A study of over 30,000 people by Richard Lucas at Michigan State University revealed that divorced people reported a permanent change in their happiness and level of distress in their lives.[7]

The longer you spend in a divorced or widowed state, the higher the likelihood of heart or lung disease, cancer, high blood pressure, diabetes, stroke and difficulties with mobility, such as walking or climbing stairs, according to the 2005 study of 8,652 people age 51 to 61.[8]

Living a full life, though, is more than physical health. It's also about personal satisfaction and fulfillment. Sixty-four percent of married people said they are very satisfied with the way their personal life is going, compared with 43% of singles.[9]

Whether you're talking about better health, greater life expectancy, more energy or just a higher level of satisfaction, marriage benefits your life in some incredible ways.

Sex

What about sex? The misconception is that only guys care about this one. But the truth is that sex is a benefit for both marriage partners—male and female. Men and women may approach sex differently, but both equally enjoy it and find fulfillment in it, when it is done within the context of marriage.

According to a survey conducted by *National Health and Social Life*, married men have sex twice as frequently as single men. Also, the married men reported higher levels of satisfaction with their own sex lives than both those who were unmarried and those who were just living with their girlfriends.[10]

Another study concluded that single guys are 20 times more likely to not have sex in a given year than their married counterparts. Single women are 10 times as likely for the same statistic.[11]

In the same study, partners who were "playing house" were more likely to get divorced, to be described as unhappy and to have sex outside of their relationship (read: cheat on their partner). According to certain studies, a couple that is playing house has a 10% shot at staying together after five years, compared to 80% of first-time, married couples.[12]

Money

Also, when we just stay married, we'll have more money. When we get married, we share the newspaper, cable bill, mortgage, electric bill and the same bed. Married people also get access to insurance savings, investment benefits and tax relief.[13] It's okay to be excited about that one!

According to *MSN® money*, married couples have immediate

access to social security benefits, pension benefits and in most states, inheritance rights as well.[14]

One study found that married men make 10-40% more money than single or cohabitating men.[15]

Remember: money is a good thing if we first bring it to God and then leverage the rest the right way. I have never met anyone who said "You know what? I just don't want any more money." If you ever meet anyone who says that, they're lying.

And if we just stay married, we will be much better off with the mean green and financial security. Don't worry about real estate or the stock market; just stay married.

Kids

Kids who grow up in stable, two-parent families have a higher standard of living, receive better parenting, are better emotionally connected to both parents and suffer fewer stressful events in their childhood.[16]

A study in Canada found that children from divorced families are twice as likely to be prescribed Ritalin.[17] The instability and stress on the children early in the transition is a likely candidate.

There are numerous benefits for children living with both parents. They are reported to have better physical health, are more successful academically and have fewer behavioral problems than those raised without both parents.[18]

The American Psychological Association (APA) supported the view that a stable family has tremendous benefits to physical and mental health than those who are raised without both mom and dad.[19]

Finally, a study by the *Daily Telegraph* in the United Kingdom stated that children from divorced homes suffer long-term financial disadvantages from those of married homes.[20]

So it's pretty obvious that your kids will benefit more from you staying married than they will from you getting divorced.

Earlier in the book, I pointed you back to Genesis to show you God's math for marriage: $1 + 1 = 1$. I talked about oneness and wholeness in this amazing relationship called marriage.

When you bail out on your marriage, what are you doing? You're halving all of your money; you're halving all of your friends; you're halving your happiness and contentment. You are halving your sexual fulfillment. You're even halving the time you can spend with your kids! You're halving everything and will end up living on fractions. It's not worth it. Do you want to live a life of fractions or a life of wholeness?

The choice is up to you through the power of God in your marriage. You either resolve to die to your needs and live for your spouse, or you don't. You either resolve to allow the power of the resurrection to do a new work in your marriage, or you don't. You just stay married or you don't.

In this chapter and throughout this book, I've given you biblical and non-biblical reasons to stay in your marriage. I truly believe that marriage between a man and a woman is the cornerstone for our society. And again, it is the only relationship that is analogous to Christ's relationship to His Church. Marriage is the greatest context in which you and your spouse can grow in your faith and show your family and the world about the power of the risen Lord.

God has an amazing agenda for you that He wants you to discover in your marriage. And so often, people quit right before the breakthrough. It's Lisa's and my fervent prayer that this book challenges you to look at yourself in the mirror and through the power of God, resolve to stay married for God's reputation, for your spouse, for your kids and yes, for you.

A TIME FOR REFLECTION

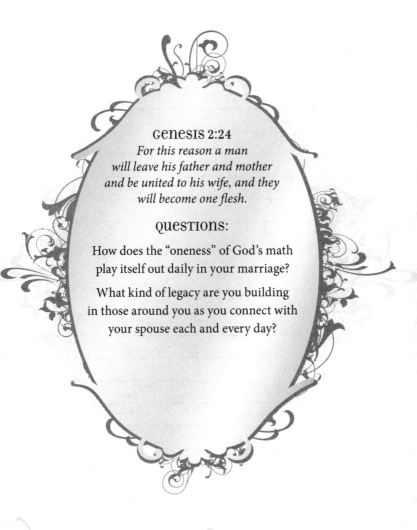

GENESIS 2:24

*For this reason a man
will leave his father and mother
and be united to his wife, and they
will become one flesh.*

QUESTIONS:

How does the "oneness" of God's math
play itself out daily in your marriage?

What kind of legacy are you building
in those around you as you connect with
your spouse each and every day?

BEYOND THE MIRROR

THEY SAID IT WAS SOMETHING CALLED AVM.

An abnormal collection of blood vessels was found on her brain. She wasn't expected to make it. While we processed the news, she laid in a hospital bed teetering between life and death.

One Wednesday night, Vanessa Whitwell was at home enjoying some well-deserved rest with her family after a particularly intense season of work and ministry. She spent the night with her father, step-mother and two sisters. Her husband, Andy, who was away on business, called to check in with her before she headed off to bed. She was set to drift off to sleep, just like any night.

She would never be the same.

Thursday morning, Vanessa was rushed to a hospital, airlifted to another hospital and later transferred to yet another hospital. A blood vessel in her brain had suddenly ruptured, sending her into a coma from which she never recovered.

Wednesday, she went to sleep like she always did. The following

Wednesday, I preached her funeral.

Vanessa Whitwell: Christ-follower, wife, daughter, sister, and a very close friend of Lisa and mine, had graduated from this life to the next. She was just 34 years of age. As I write this, I still struggle to attach the past tense to her name.

Over the ensuing days, as my family, church and friends processed this sudden tragedy, we cried a lot. We celebrated such a beautiful life in Vanessa. We knew, and still know, that she is home with her heavenly Father. But we still had tons of questions and faced a lot of confusing emotions. But mostly, we hurt for Andy.

How was I going to preach at the funeral of someone who was in the prime of her life? Someone who, for the last twelve years, had been the wife and best friend of my own very good friend? What could I possibly say to help or heal? As I thought about what I was going to say, my mind raced back to a recent trip to Hawaii we shared with Andy and Vanessa.

There's something unique about travelling with another couple. With all the stress of air travel these days, it's very difficult to mask our true feelings and natural reactions. You quickly find out the real deal about someone when you travel with them. You can see if their walk and talk connect; if they are just putting on the show, or showing you their real stuff. So as Lisa and I traveled with the Whitwell's, we got to peak behind the reflective glass, beyond the mirror of their marriage.

The odds were stacked against Andy and Vanessa from the beginning. If you'd looked behind the mirror of their marriage from the world's view, you wouldn't have thought they could make it. Both came from broken homes. And that inherited legacy of family dysfunction created major obstacles long after Andy and Vanessa said "I do".

Together, they battled substance abuse.

Together, they faced the hurdle and difficulty of infertility.

Together they battled the temptation to dive headlong into their careers—him a successful business executive; her a vital part of the ministry of Fellowship Church.

On paper, the odds were overwhelming. And yet, their marriage was an example to us all; because together they reflected the grace and power of God in their marriage. Together.

On that trip to Hawaii, we saw the true image that their mirror reflected. One morning, we were all swimming in the ocean. And I remember these huge, *Hawaii Five-O* type waves; the kind that tower above you and crash all around you. The last place I wanted to be was in the middle of those waves. Most of us were content to stay a few feet from shore to protect ourselves from the angry surf. But not Vanessa.

As I looked to my left, I saw Vanessa swimming out to meet these monster waves head-on. She wasn't content to get her feet wet; she wanted to totally immerse herself in the Hawaii surf experience. Because of the challenges she faced on a daily basis, Vanessa was used to meeting monstrous obstacles like these Hawaiian waves. And Andy had a lot to do with her ability to fight them. And he knew and understood her strength and her desire to live life to the fullest.

When I looked at Andy and asked, "Man, what is she doing?!" He simply looked at me and said, "You know Vanessa. Go big or don't go at all!"

There are some experiences that mark you and change you forever. Some friendships are so special that they can never be replaced. Andy and Vanessa's marriage typified what the marriage mirror is all about. Their example was a major catalyst for this book. Our friendship with the Andy and Vanessa provided Lisa and me with a vivid and unmistakable picture of God's relationship with His Church. Their marriage typified the amazing results that come from the reflection of the gospel through a man and woman in the marital covenant. Go big, or don't go at all.

Andy and Vanessa could have thrown in the towel on so many occasions. Most couples would have bailed if they had to face what the Whitwell's faced. But Andy and Vanessa weren't most couples. Both of them had made a commitment to Jesus Christ—a commitment that played itself out in the context of their marriage. Their love wasn't based on "if you do this, I'll do this" type conditions. It wasn't built on fleeting feelings. Their marriage was difficult; every marriage is. But in the end, Andy and Vanessa used their marriage to reflect the death, burial and resurrection of Jesus Christ unlike many other marriages I have seen.

In the waiting room at the hospital, as Vanessa lie stranded between this life and eternity, Andy told Lisa and me something that I will never forget. In his calm, southern drawl, Andy spoke with words that could only be described as supernatural in that particular moment. As we all reflected on their marriage and life together, Andy leaned forward and said, with tears in his eyes, "You know, I always knew that God had given Vanessa to me for just a season."

Here was a man facing the reality of losing his young wife. But all he could think of and talk about was the gift of having Vanessa—even if it was for a short time.

It was a short sentence that captured so much emotion and feeling. And it was just one more intimate glimpse into their marriage; a rare opportunity to peak behind the mirror and see its true nature. Knowing that Andy and Vanessa's marriage was built by and for Christ made all the difference.

Lisa and I learned many valuable lessons from their marriage. It was so inspirational for us to see a couple overcome the many odds that were stacked against them. It was so inspirational to see a couple fight to stay united through the pressures and the stresses that befall so many other marriages. Because of their connection to Christ and the hard work they put in to overcome obstacles together, they truly achieved the oneness that the Bible talks about.

To know Vanessa was to know Andy and to know Andy was to know Vanessa. You could not separate them. They took nothing for granted in their relationship. They were intentional with one another as they faced each day. And through it all, they showcased and reflected the death, burial and resurrection of Jesus.

The Whitwells' marriage was phenomenal. It was the kind of marriage that wasn't made in Hollywood; it was too authentic for the silver screen. The marriage that Lisa and I saw in Andy and Vanessa was only made through the grace of Jesus Christ through their commitment to the gospel and to one another. Theirs was a supernatural marriage. And that's the reflection the world saw.

WHaT DO YOU See?

I would be remiss if I did not end this book with a challenge that goes above and beyond marriage. I've talked a lot about what the Bible says about the work it takes to have a God-centered marriage throughout this book. But the work between a husband and a wife is only supernatural when both people have allowed the work of Christ to be reflected in their personal lives. As I preached Vanessa's funeral, I made sure that I captured the opportunity to articulate the one thing that marked Andy and Vanessa's marriage:

the gospel. I want to offer the same opportunity to you.

Do you have that love relationship with Jesus Christ? Or are you trying to jump through certain hoops to appease our holy God? What Vanessa had was a grace reception through the finished work of Jesus Christ.

Marriage might be spelled w-o-r-k, but Christianity is spelled d-o-n-e; Jesus has done the work. He died, He was buried, He has risen again and He offers you this abundant life today and an eternal life for tomorrow.[1]

Other philosophies and religions are spelled d-o; they are based on what you can and can't do. But the problem is that you and I can't do enough or be good enough or polish the mirror enough to ever see God in our lives.

You either receive the free gift of salvation from Jesus Christ, or you try to do your own thing. Have you personally made that grace reception?

How about your marriage? Do you see God reflected in the only relationship that mirrors His relationship to His people? As you look at your marriage, do you see the death, burial and resurrection reflected back to you? Do you see a love, a power that is on tap that only comes from God Himself? A rich, full life and marriage are waiting for you…if you just take a look in the mirror.

endnotes

Chapter 1

1. Ezekiel 16:8-14
2. Jeremiah 3:20
3. Hosea 2:9-10
4. Ephesians 5:25
5. Genesis 2:24
6. 1 Corinthians 15:32
7. Ephesians 1:15-22
8. Romans 5:8
9. 1 Peter 1:15-16
10. "The Sacred Marriage" by Gary Thomas (Zondervan, 2000)

Chapter 2

1. James 1:23-24
2. Matthew 22:37-40
3. Luke 23:34
4. Ephesians 5:25
5. 2 Peter 1:5-7

Chapter 3

1. Genesis 1:28
2. Genesis 2:24
3. 1 Corinthians 7:9
4. 1 Corinthians 7:5
5. 1 Corinthians 7:3, 4
6. Proverbs 27:17
7. Genesis 1:1
8. Revelation 21:5

Chapter 4

1. Colossians 3:23
2. Romans 12:1
3. 1 Corinthians 6:19-20
4. Genesis 1:26-27
5. Ephesians 5:25
6. Ephesians 5:23
7. For a more in depth look at authority in marriage, see the marriage series "Authority Issues" on EdYoung.com
8. 2 Corinthians 5:18
9. John 3:16
10. Ephesians 5:33

Chapter 5

1. James 4:14
2. Song of Solomon 2:1
3. Time Magazine, "Marry Me" (Thursday, Jan. 17, 2008) by LORI OLIWENSTEIN
   http://www.time.com/time/magazine/article/0,9171,1704686-1,00.html
4. Ibid.
5. *US News and World Report*; "Happy Marriage, Happy Heart", March 20, 2008; http://health.
   usnews.com/usnews/health/healthday/080320/happy-marriage-happy-heart.htm
6. *United Press International*, "Divorced Men at Greater Risk", Copenhagen, Denmark
   (June 1, 2006) http://www.365reasons.com/health.htm
7. "Divorce Makes People Miserable for Life" by Amelia Hill. In The Guardian UK - *The Observer*
   January 8, 2006; http://www.365reasons.com/health.htm
8. "Another Argument for Marriage" by Sue Shellenbarger; *The Wall Street Journal*,
   June 16, 2005 http://www.365reasons.com/health.htm
9. "Marriage Beats Money for Happiness" by Jennifer Warner for WebMD Health News,
   January 4, 2007.
10. "Studies Find Big Benefits in Marriage" by Jennifer Steinhauer; *New York Times*: Health
    (April 10, 1995).
11. "Why Marriage is Good for You" by Maggie Gallagher, City Journal, (Autumn, 2000);
    http://www.catholiceducation.org/articles/marriage/mf0029.html
12. Ibid.
13. "Five Ways to Save Money Through Marriage" by Duffy Winters for "The Motley Fool"
    http://www.fool.com/specials/2000/sp000907.htm
14. "The Myth of the Marriage Penalty" in *MSN money* by Liz Pulliam Weston;
    June 2, 2008 http://articles.moneycentral.msn.com/CollegeAndFamily/LoveAndMoney/
    TheMythOfTheMarriagePenalty.aspx?page=1
15. "The Many Benefits of Traditional Marriage" by Sara Russo for Accuracy in America,
    December, 2000; http://www.academia.org/campus_reports/2000/december_2000_4.html
16. Marriage Matters for Children – Research, Press Release: Family First, July 4, 2007, Media
    Release
17. "Children of Divorce Twice as Likely to be Put on Ritalin" The Star, Edmonton, Canada by
    Helen Branswell, June 06, 2007, Canadian Press.
18. A Marriage of Family and Education: Stable Home Life Helps Children Learn; Zenit News
    Service (zenit.org) January 14, 2006
19. Effects of Parental Support During Childhood, American Psychological Association,
    March 21, 2004
20. "Children of Married Parents Do Better in Life" *Daily Telegraph* (UK); Sarah Womack,
    Social Affairs, December 12, 2003.

Chapter 6

1   John 10:10

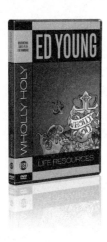

Creative Marriage Book

Disposable relationships and throw away marriages permeate our culture. When the dream fades and the realities of life set in, many just throw in the towel. In their book, *The Creative Marriage: The Art of Keeping Your Love Alive*, Ed and Lisa Young take a penetrating look at what it means to have a lasting marriage in today's world.

Creative Marriage Study Guide

In this **6-part** study, Ed and Lisa help you take a revealing look at what it means to have a lasting marriage in today's world. From communication and conflict resolution to making sound financial decisions and effective parenting, creativity is a necessary element that should permeate every aspect of your relationship.